£4

Wish You Were Here, Jimmy Dean

Wish You Were Here, Jimmy Dean

James Dean recalled in words and pictures

Martin Dawber

COLUMBUS BOOKS
LONDON

Dedication
This book is for Carole with love

Many friends and colleagues helped in the preparation
and research of this book. Among them were Sylvia
Bongiovani, Gabi Bader, Jacques de Montrosty, Bo
Ivander, Kenneth Kendall, David Loehr, Enrico Perego,
Norman Patterson, Mark Roesler, and members of
'We Remember James Dean International'.
I would also like to thank The James Dean Foundation,
c/o Curtis Management Group, Indianapolis, USA.

First published in Great Britain in 1988 by
Columbus Books Limited
19-23 Ludgate Hill, London EC4M 7PD

Designed by Paperweight
Phototypeset by Falcon Graphic Art Ltd
Wallington, Surrey
Printed and bound by arrangement with
Graphicom SRL, Vicenza, Italy

British Library Cataloguing in Publication Data
Dawber, Martin
Wish You Were Here, Jimmy Dean
    1. Cinema films. Acting. Dean, James, 1931–55.
Biographies.
    I. Dawber, Martin
791.43'028'0924
    ISBN 0 86287 388 6

Contents

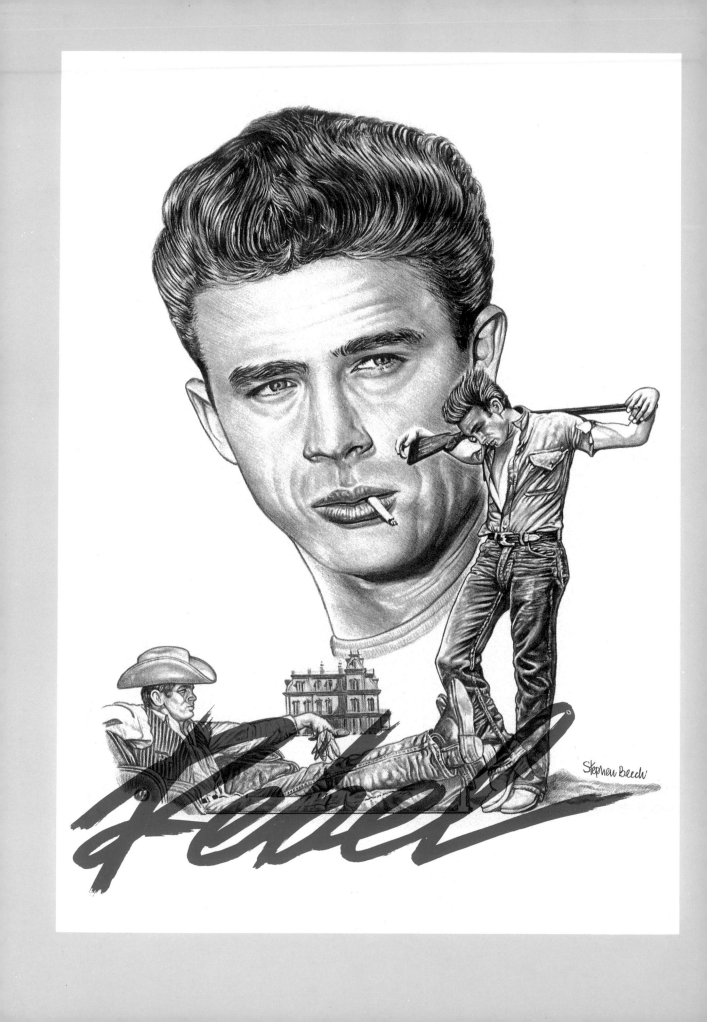

Stephen Beech

Introduction

'And now here is my secret, a very simple
secret: it is only with the heart that one can see
rightly; what is essential is invisible to the eye.'

The Little Prince, *Antoine de Saint-Exupéry*

*J*ames Dean is a phenomenon: to a generation of followers
he is an icon, whose reputation rests today on the three
major films he completed before his death in 1955 – *Rebel Without
a Cause*, *East of Eden* and *Giant*. Thirty years on, the legend is still
with us, in the written testimonies of those who knew him and the
graphic representations of artists inspired by his memory.

The screen persona remains as potent today as it was in the 'fifties.
Every facet of Dean the man, the actor, the myth, has been fully
catalogued by the faithful and the curious alike in the years after his
death. He has never lost his status as 'the first American teenager',
the eternal rebel – someone with whom the outsider and social misfit
can often feel immediate empathy. It seems probable that more
words have been put on paper about Dean's career than that of
almost any other star – which is all the more remarkable given his
comet-like existence.

At 24 he was dead, but his presence left its mark in the memories
of those whose lives he had touched. Whatever one's speculations
about Dean the actor, he brought to the screen the personification of
the confused teenager thirty years before the 'Brat Pack' recreated it
in the 'eighties. In one package, he provided the focus for all the
generation-gap hang-ups of succeeding years.

His early death in an automobile accident trapped him in time.
Though his contemporaries included John Garfield and Montgomery
Clift, Marlon Brando and Paul Newman, it was Dean who stole

forever the mantle of immortality. Confirmation of his status required, or so many have claimed, the ultimate sacrifice. Death enshrined him as a figurehead.

Dean was as fascinating off screen as on. Consciously or not, the viewer identifies instantly with the misunderstood kid, the loner, the doubting, brooding adolescent bent on self-destruction. His life takes on new meaning in the media of paint and canvas. For three decades artists have risen to the challenge of capturing Dean on paper and canvas, as if to compensate for the limited celluloid footage he left us, and thus the flame has been kept ever-bright. Deanobilia has kept James Dean eternally young and ever-present in our lives. His image is emblazoned on posters and T-shirts, camouflages bedroom walls, falls through letter-boxes, hangs in galleries, accosts us from the pages of books and magazines.

Many artists have found something inspirational in the symbol of Dean: the transience of youth, and the inevitability of death. Paint on paper holds his image as film once captured and preserved it.

And perhaps the face reflected back at them is as much a self-portrait as it is a likeness of Dean.

1
The Beginnings, 1931-54

'And, if you should come upon this spot, please do not hurry on. Wait for a time, exactly under the star. Then, if a little man appears who laughs, who has golden hair and who refuses to answer questions, you will know who he is.'

The Little Prince, *Antoine de Saint-Exupéry*

ate: 8 February 1931. Location: Green Gables Apartments, 320 East Fourth Street, Marion, Indiana, USA. Time: 2 a.m. The birth of the only child of Winton Dean and his 21-year-old wife, Mildred Wilson Dean, was a difficult home delivery for the local doctor, James Emmick. In gratitude, the Deans named their son after him. They also chose 'Byron', after Mildred's favourite poet, and in due course their son was christened James Byron Dean.

Times were rough for the Deans, and four years later, in July 1935, the family was forced to uproot itself – first to a farm at Fairmount, ten miles south of Marion, owned by Winton's sister and brother-in-law, Ortense and Marcus Winslow, and then to California, three thousand miles away, where Winton Dean had taken a job as a dental technician at a Santa Monica hospital.

During those early years James Dean was drawn into a claustrophobic relationship with his mother and was surrounded by a protective barrier of her making. Her own artistic leanings were brought to bear on Jimmy from an early age. She read him poetry, played the piano to him, acted out plays with him in a toy theatre built from a cardboard box, and had him take both tap-dancing and piano lessons. In time she acquired a child's violin for him. Over-protective and vicariously ambitious, Mildred cocooned her son throughout his formative years.

When he entered Brentwood Public School, he was shy and awkward with his classmates, who sneered at his violin and would refer to him as James Byron, instead of calling him by the family nickname 'Deanie'. (In adulthood he disowned his middle name.)

Early in 1938 Mildred Dean was diagnosed as having advanced breast cancer, and Winton was eventually obliged to sell the family home to meet the hospital bills. He found it difficult to answer his son's questions and an impenetrable curtain of silence imposed itself between father and son. Jimmy blamed his father for not making his mother well. In the spring of 1940, advised that his wife had only about six weeks to live, Winton asked his mother, Emma, to come to Los Angeles to look after Jimmy.

On 14 April Mildred Dean died and the gulf between father and son widened. His financial resources exhausted, Winton was unable to afford the fare to accompany his wife's body back to Indiana, nor could he drive to Marion, having already been forced to sell the family car. On the suggestion of his mother, he sent the body with Jimmy and his grandmother. Winton's sister would look after her young nephew on their 400-acre farm at Fairmount while Winton sorted out his life in California. So ended his emotional ties to the son he had never really understood – a break that was further reinforced in 1942 when Dean Senior was drafted into the Army Medical Corps.

On 20 April 1940 young Jimmy, who to all intents and purposes had been orphaned, travelled back to Indiana on the same train as his mother's coffin, there to be fostered at the Winslow homestead. As funeral arrangements were being made, Jimmy crept downstairs and took a ribbon from one of the wreaths on the coffin. It remained beneath his pillow for a long time.

For several months Jimmy, a natural introvert, was too traumatized to settle into his new home or to form a relationship with his aunt and uncle, or with his cousin Joan, two years his senior, and he often withdrew into unnerving silence.

Life on the Winslows' farm was very different from Jimmy's past life. He helped with the livestock and day-to-day running of the place, and in time settled into a routine. This helped drive away some of his melancholy, but there were still days of silence. Ortense and Marcus Winslow treated Jimmy as if he were their own child, and for his tenth birthday they gave him a pony: he always loved animals. He was also introduced to the joys of driving – on the farm's tractor. When Jimmy was twelve, the Winslows, whom Jimmy now called 'Mom' and 'Dad', had another child, a son they named Marcus Jr. This made Jimmy the Winslow orphan again, the label he had had such trouble trying to shrug off. He tried to work off some of his misery in school athletics, and at home his uncle installed a trapeze for him: he was in fact proving to be something of an athlete. Workout was to prove costly, however: one day he hit the barn door and knocked out his front two teeth. From then on he wore two false front teeth on a brace.

Jimmy was soon given his first motorcycle, really a souped-up bicycle fitted with a lawn-mower engine, which he drove erratically round the farm – breaking four pairs of spectacles in as many weeks. He graduated to a used 125cc motorbike from Marvin Carter's Fairmount bike shop and became a racing fanatic, tearing round a dirt-track he had laid out in a field behind the store. On his bigger bike Jimmy was able to do up to 50 mph, and earned himself the nickname of 'One-speed Dean'. His mentor was the town's Wesleyan minister, the Rev. James De-Weerd, who had been approached by Jimmy's aunt for guidance when Jimmy started collapsing into his silent state. A Second World War veteran, De-Weerd shared and encouraged Jimmy's new interest in motor-racing and took him to Indianapolis for the famous '500' race.

At Fairmount High School, Jimmy was a bright student, both academically and on the sports field, showing particular prowess in basketball and baseball. He was gifted in art but took most pride in becoming president of the school's Thespian Society. He would walk out into his uncle's fields and recite at the top of his voice to a bewildered audience of grazing cattle in the hope of overcoming his fear of performing in public. Human audiences could be more difficult: when his seventh-grade classmates sniggered one day at a poem he was reading in class Jimmy's whiplash response caused a major brawl that brought him several days' suspension. His yearning to act had not gone unnoticed by his aunt, who directed his energies to better use at her local Women's Christian Temperance Union meetings. Here he delivered his own tongue-in-cheek speeches on 'the demon drink'.

In a high school parody, *Goon with the Wind*, Jimmy played Frankenstein's monster as well as other roles in school plays. For the 1949 drama contest sponsored by the National Forensic League his text was *A Madman's Manuscript*, an adaptation of Charles Dickens' *Pickwick Papers*. His performance, featuring several bloodcurdling screams, won him his state heat, which entitled him to enter the National Finals in Longmont, Colorado on 30 April. His coach Adeline Hall warned him that the speech needed trimming, but Jimmy ignored her and was duly disqualified for going two minutes over the ten-minute limit. His bitterness at not winning made him doubt whether acting was his true *métier*.

James Dean graduated on 16 May 1949, scholastically 'above average' but 'handicapped by a lack of application'. He was awarded the school's athletics medal and a prize for art, but his grades prevented his going on to college. His prospects looked bleak.

As a stop-gap, Jimmy applied to law school, on his father's suggestion, and was accepted by Santa Monica Community College on condition that he enrol on a summer cramming course. After hurried goodbyes to the Winslows, Jimmy boarded the silver Greyhound bus on 15 June for the journey west, apprehensive at the prospect of joining his father and unknown stepmother in their Santa Monica home. The reunion between father and son failed to stir any familial affection. While waiting for term to start, Jimmy joined the local summer stock company and took part in a musical, *The Romance of Scarlet Gulch*, using the stage name Byron James. Winton Dean had little sympathy with his son's ambition to act.

On 18 January 1950, the 18-year-old James Dean began his freshman year, but found little in the law to excite his imagination. He took drama classes in his spare time, and worked as an announcer on the college's radio station. After a few months of study he enrolled as a drama student at the University of California in Los Angeles for the forthcoming autumn term and took rooms nearby.

After dropping out of Santa Monica, Jimmy spent the summer recess earning money from part-time jobs. For a time he worked as an athletics instructor in a local military academy, then went back to Indiana to help his uncle gather in the harvest. One night he drove into Marion to catch a new movie which everyone was talking about: it featured Marlon Brando's film début, in Fred Zinnemann's *The Men*, and Brando's performance had him riveted to his seat. He returned to California in the autumn of 1950 determined to become a great actor.

UCLA boasted the best-equipped theatre arts department in the state, for it was able to borrow props and costumes from some of the neighbouring film studios. UCLA's major autumn production was to be Shakespeare's *Macbeth*. Jimmy played Malcolm, and his performance caught the eye of a Burbank talent scout, Isabel Draesmer, who thought she detected more in James Dean than Shakespeare was able to bring out. Afterwards, she suggested that armed with some good photographs he would do well to visit the local casting offices.

Jimmy's professional screen début came a year later, thanks to Draesmer, now his agent, in a one-and-a-half-minute Pepsi-Cola commercial filmed in Griffith Park – scene of many a cowboy-and-Indian chase in the old Hollywood westerns. Along with other young amateurs, Nick Adams and Beverley Long, he sang, 'Pepsi-Cola hits the spot. . .' Curiously, all three would later return to this location for the filming of *Rebel Without a Cause*. Jimmy was paid $30 for the two days' shooting.

However, in January 1951, depressed by his failure to win a role in the College's spring production, Jimmy withdrew from UCLA. James Whitmore, a UCLA tutor who had studied at the New York Actors' Studio, was organizing some informal acting classes in an empty room over the Brentwood Country Mart. This was all the tutoring Dean felt he needed. Whitmore taught his group the Stanislavski 'Method' which had so impressed Jimmy when he saw Brando act.

In the meantime, Jerry Fairbanks, the producer of the Pepsi-Cola commercial, signed Jimmy for the part of John the Baptist in an Easter television special. With only a handful of lines, Jimmy's part in *Hill Number One* was not particularly memorable, yet his screen charisma was such that some girls at a local Catholic school formed the Immaculate Heart James Dean Appreciation Society soon after the broadcast. But before long their hero, in financial difficulties again, had withdrawn into himself. He drifted aimlessly through each day, his only anchor Whitmore's study group, to which he remained dedicated. A job as a uniformed car attendant at the local CBS Radio Studios was short-lived: he was soon fired for looking too untidy. His 'uniform' of T-shirts and jeans was already established.

His moods were beginning to affect his long-standing friendship with his room-mate Bill Bast. Matters finally came to a head when they both fell for the same girl, and for a while Jimmy moved out.

Bit parts in films and occasional radio spots kept the wolf from the

door. In his first film, *Fixed Bayonets*, directed by Sam Fuller, his only line ('It's the rearguard coming back') was cut. He flashed by in close-up as a sultry sailor in a Dean Martin/Jerry Lewis comedy, *Sailors Beware*, and was an extra in *Trouble Along the Way*, starring John Wayne. In *Has Anybody Seen My Girl?* he delivered the immortal words 'Hey, Gramps, I'll have a chocolate malt, heavy on the choc, plenty of milk, four spoons of malt, two scoops of vanilla ice cream, one mixed and one floating'. It was his longest line on film in 1951.

Rogers Brackett, a young radio producer at CBS, secured some radio parts for Jimmy and put him up for a few weeks, during which Jimmy encountered the Hollywood cocktail circuit for the first time and found it superficial and false. He was hungry for challenging work and desperately wanted to go to New York, join the Actors' Studio and try for Broadway. Armed with a letter of recommendation and a list of contacts from Brackett, Jimmy left a message for Bill Bast, with whom he had patched up his quarrel: 'Mr Dean called. Gone to New York.'

He reached Manhattan in September 1951, moved into the YMCA and withdrew into his shell. His main pastime was to watch films in the 24-hour cinemas. Within a few weeks, having spent $150 on movie-going, he took a job in a drug-store and moved into cheaper lodgings in a hotel off Times Square. Eventually, following up Brackett's contacts, he began the humiliating round of producers' and agents' offices, but no one seemed interested in yet another out-of-town fledgling. However, at the Louis Schurr Agency he was interviewed by Schurr's assistant Jane Deacy, who, in common with Adeline Nall and Isabel Draesmer before her, detected something different in Jimmy and took him on to her books. A guiding light had entered his life. Jane Deacy was to encourage him and direct his career right up until his death.

He began inauspiciously with the job of pre-testing the competitions on TV's game show *Beat the Clock*, at $5 an hour. Better offers were slow to materialize. In May he took a room with

Bill Bast again, at the Iroquois Hotel on West 44th Street, at $90 a month. Jimmy's days were spent at casting sessions, but the small parts he played on radio and television frustrated him and earned him a reputation for being difficult to work with. Producers became impatient at the length of time he took to prepare even the smallest role. He was becoming his own worst enemy.

Then there was that lingering ambition to join the Actors' Studio – a precious but frightening goal. Eventually, after four weeks' preparation with another of Jane Deacy's clients, Christine White, he presented himself before Lee Strasberg on 12 November: they were two out of a total of 150 candidates for the 1952 entrance examination. Their 15-minute drama, *Ripping Off Layers to Find Roots*, was performed only after the petrified Jimmy had run round the block to burn off his adrenalin. Both were picked to go forward and the following day only Jimmy and Christine, from a shortlist of twelve, were chosen.

The Actors' Studio had been formed in 1947 by Cheryl Crawford and Elia Kazan to replace the dying American Theatre Group of the 1930s. In 1952 the studio was presided over by Lee and Molly Strasberg. Lee Strasberg, a hard disciplinarian, would tear actors to shreds in analysing their performances. Although familiar with the philosophy of the Method school from his days in James Whitmore's drama classes, Jimmy was totally unprepared for Strasberg's verbal attacks.

The first time Jimmy faced one of his onslaughts he walked out, vowing never to return. He was too insecure to reveal his 'Achilles' heel' in the way that Strasberg demanded.

Winter was drawing on. Jimmy worked on a Hudson River tugboat then hitched back to Fairmount to spend Thanksgiving with his aunt and uncle. The warmth and comfort of the old, familiar surroundings brought him peace of mind and gave him a few days in which to question his aims in life. Then, once again, fate stepped in.

Earlier in the year Jimmy had heard about producer Lemuel Ayers' plan to mount Richard Nash's *See the Jaguar* on Broadway. With help from Deacy, Jimmy had met Ayers to discuss the project. Suddenly he was called to audition for the role of the confused delinquent Wally Watkins, which he and Deacy felt was tailor-made for him. He got the part and, after the preliminary out-of-town run, in Hartford, Connecticut, James Dean cut his Broadway teeth at the Court Theatre, New York, on 3 December 1952. The audience was enthusiastic, but the critics slammed the play and it closed after only six performances. However, Jimmy's own performance carried enough weight to bring offers of better roles in television playlets and soaps. He bought a British Triumph 500 motorbike, on which he shot across New York from studio to studio. Jane Deacy took a firm stand over the parts he should accept (mainly misunderstood juvenile leads), and Jimmy found himself established as one of the 1950s 'brat-pack' (fellow members Paul Newman and Steve McQueen). Sacks of fan-mail began to arrive at the Schurr office. By October he was starring in Rod Serling's *A Long Time Till Dawn* for the prestigious NBC Kraft TV Theatre. A review in *Variety* prompted an audition from MGM scouts, but Deacy steered Jimmy away from facile Hollywood parts. Even the offer of a starring role in a Cinemascope epic called *The Silver Chalice* could not dissuade her. Meanwhile, Jimmy's television work went from strength to strength and his face was becoming well known.

Between acting jobs he spent time with a new circle of friends, including the musician Leonard Rosenman who would later score both *East of Eden* and *Rebel Without a Cause*, took photography lessons with Roy Schatt, studied modern ballet and dance with Kathleen Dunham and began developing his jazz interests, learning to play the bongo drums in Greenwich Village folk cellars. But his outward demeanour was belied by the feeling of isolation that so easily overcame him when he was not working, and by insomniac nights spent roaming the New York city streets.

In late 1953 Jimmy got his second Broadway role – Bakir, an Arab house-boy in André Gide's autobiographical work *The Immoralist*, in which a honeymooning archaeologist (Louis Jourdan) breaks down under the strain of admitting his homosexuality to his wife, played by Geraldine Page.

Jimmy took trouble to make his part believable. He biked 800 miles home to Fairmount to study T.E. Lawrence's *Seven Pillars of Wisdom*, seeking insight into the Arab psyche. But his dedication caused friction between him and the rest of the company and created a bad atmosphere backstage, especially when he arrived late for rehearsals. Despite good press, his part was heavily cut after the Philadelphia preview, and Jimmy had a major row with his producer, Billy Rose, a week before the New York opening at the Royale. Confused and upset, Jimmy walked out of a rehearsal, only to suffer the humiliation, when he returned, of seeing his understudy reading his part.

The première brought lukewarm press notices for the play but praise for his own performance – which later earned him the Daniel Blunt Theatre Award for most promising newcomer of the year and a Tony award as best supporting actor of 1954. Jimmy, believing he had been cheated and could trust no one, handed in his two-week notice to quit. However, Jane Deacy persuaded Elia Kazan, then in New York casting for his screen adaptation of John Steinbeck's *East of Eden*, to catch Jimmy's performance. Impressed, Kazan invited Jimmy to audition.

In Hollywood it had been rumoured that Montgomery Clift and Marlon Brando would be cast as the Trask brothers, but in New York the running had now been narrowed to three younger actors: Richard Davalos, Paul Newman and Jimmy Dean. Kazan had encountered Jimmy at the Actors' Studio the previous year, even riding pillion on his motorcycle, and soon decided that Dean would be ideal casting for Cal Trask.

Jane Deacy secured a $20,000 contract for Jimmy against an advance of $4,000. When he headed back to Hollywood he was no longer a struggling bit-player but an accomplished actor with the film role of the year. On 8 March, with Kazan, Jimmy boarded a plane for the first time, heading for California and screen history.

2
East of Eden

*'I've got to know who I am. I've got to know
what I'm like. I've got to know.'*

Cal Trask in *East of Eden*, 1955

The initial shooting of *East of Eden* was scheduled to begin on 27 May 1954 in Mendocino, California. This gave Jimmy two weeks to find his feet and he spent it on a ranch in Borrego Springs. The advance from Warner Brothers enabled Jimmy to indulge his passion for racing by buying a red MG sports car and his love of animals by acquiring a palomino horse. The ranch proved a welcome sanctuary from prying West Coast journalists, eager to suss out the latest rival to Clift and Brando, and also from the Hollywood socialites, most of whom he remembered from his auditioning days. Slightly more at ease now, he spent a few days soaking up the sun, lounging around in jeans and T-shirt, riding his palomino or practising his lariat technique. Among the familiar faces were Nick Adams, from the Pepsi-Cola commercial, Joseph Wiseman and Paul Newman. Newman introduced Jimmy as his New York shadow and endeared himself still less by presenting Jimmy's break into big-time movies as one of acting's all-time lucky breaks. Jimmy soon found himself hounded by gossipmongers eager to play up the Brando comparison. Under pressure, he challenged Brando to an acting duel and began shooting his mouth off in front of the press. In a further act of rebellion, Jimmy ignored Warner Brothers' ban on riding motorbikes and bought a new, more powerful, model.

The *Eden* screenplay began two-thirds of the way into Steinbeck's novel and concentrated on the parallels with Cain and Abel in the characters of the brothers, Cal and Aron (Richard Davalos). They are dominated by their father (Raymond Massey), a puritanical figure significantly named Adam. Cal is fated to discover that their mother, Kate (Jo Van Fleet) is not dead as their father would have them believe, but is running a brothel in nearby Monterey. In an attempt to emulate his brother and gain his father's love, Cal borrows $5000 from his mother to invest in a crop-raising scheme with one of his father's business colleagues. With the First World War imminent, the profits of the harvest are guaranteed and will enable Cal to pay his father back the money he lost on a previous food refrigeration/transportation venture. Cal offers the sum to his father as a birthday present, aided in the enterprise by Abra (Julie Harris), Aron's girlfriend, who has begun to transfer her affections to Cal. Adam rejects the gift, accusing his son of profiteering at the expense of the already exploited farmers. The rejection provokes a crisis, and Cal confronts his brother with their supposedly dead mother at the brothel. Aron, his dreams shattered, and angry at the obviously mutual attraction of Cal and Abra, casts aside his previous pacifist views and after a drinking bout enlists in the army. Adam suffers a stroke at the news. Only when Abra pleads for him to acknowledge and love his son Cal is a reconciliation effected.

The part of Cal provided Jimmy with the means of working out some of his inner conflicts in public: his mother's 'desertion', by her death, and his distant relationship with his father. Jimmy's ability to convey rejection was the special quality Kazan had first noticed in him; the young man's grudge against Winton Dean and his subsequent lonely, unstable existence had given Jimmy precisely the sort of defensive, vulnerable demeanour Kazan wanted.

The young actor found these early days back in Hollywood and the strain of this major film role extremely difficult to cope with; at Brando's suggestion Jimmy consulted a psychiatrist, but this gave him little comfort. His anti-social behaviour seemed to stem from a desperate craving for attention. Full of self-pity and doubt, he found it difficult to form any stable relationships, feeling he could give little in return for love or friendship. Instead, he took delight in provocative antics, a scruffy appearance, coarse language, non-co-operation on the set, and keeping a Colt .45 and knives in his jacket.

When shooting in Mendocino had finished, in June, the film unit moved to Salinas. Location shooting was complete by the 11th, when the unit moved into Warner Brothers' studios for the indoor scenes. Paul Newman, now viewed as a rival, was shooting MGM's *The Silver Chalice* on the adjoining sound stage and Jimmy was curious to see him at work. However, Newman's co-star, the 21-year-old starlet Pier Angeli, proved to be of greater interest, and very soon they had started a passionate love affair, much to the displeasure of Pier's overbearing mother. They spent their free time together at a rented beach house. Jimmy confided in Pier far more than he had done with any other person. The days they spent relaxing on the beach, away from the gossip columnists, were idyllic for Jimmy, but as head of a strict Catholic family, Pier's mother mother took a dim view of this Quaker with the reputation of a rebel courting her daughter.

On 13 August, the last reel of *East of Eden* was shot, to sighs of relief from most of the unit. Under pressure from Pier's family, Jimmy had become frightened and even more insecure, and his behaviour on the set more difficult to control. Kazan tried to help by suggesting that they share adjoining dressing rooms on the lot as 'homes' for the rest of the movie. He persuaded Warner Brothers to waive their ruling against live-in dressing rooms for employees, believing that closer proximity day and night might help Jimmy. However, nursing the unstable actor was beginning to take its toll on the long-suffering Kazan, and he could sense his paternal feelings rapidly dissipating.

Jimmy didn't want the movie to end. What for the others was the light at the end of the tunnel seemed for him like an oncoming train. The filming completed, Jimmy slumped into a deep depression. Afraid to face the outside world, he made his dressing room into a hermit's cell. One evening, wandering across the now-empty stages, he stumbled unwittingly into the studio head, Jack Warner. After a heated and abusive exchange of words, Jimmy was given twelve hours to pack his bags and leave the lot. After vandalizing studio property during the night, he moved out into an apartment in the Los Angeles suburb of Sherman Oaks. He bought a new motorcycle and worked off his frustration by racing up and down Sunset Boulevard.

Towards the end of September, Jimmy returned to New York for an NBC TV Playhouse production. While he was out of town, Mama Angeli went into action. There was soon talk of a new man in her daughter's life and, in October, Pier Angeli announced her engagement to the singer Vic Damone, who was both Italian and Catholic. Deeply shocked at the news, Jimmy withdrew into a black mood and tried to distract himself with one-night stands. The wedding, held on 24 November at the Westwood Church, turned into a big Hollywood social event. Jimmy, naturally uninvited, waited outside astride his motorcycle. When the bride and groom appeared, he revved his engine, drowning out the celebration bells, and sped out of Los Angeles.

When he reappeared in Hollywood two weeks later, driving a Porsche Speedster (a trade-in for his MG), the editing of *East of Eden* was nearing completion. Watching the rushes in October, Warner Brothers had recognized Jimmy's star quality and extended his contract for a further nine films over the next six years. Meanwhile the publicity department feverishly set about promoting this new screen sensation. Jimmy had no intention of co-operating, but his refusal to provide them with personal details and 'stories' only provoked a spate of scandalmongering in the tabloids. He was sarcastic to journalists, who egged him on to more sensational acts. Once he pulled his newly framed portrait down from the wall and smashed it on the studio floor. Hedda Hopper denounced him, but whatever the press said, nothing could detract from his magnetism on screen.

Sneak previews of *Eden* in Hollywood were receiving rave receptions. He was being hailed as the most powerful new talent since Marlon Brando and praise for his performance was unanimous. He heard about all this from his old fifth-floor apartment on 68th Street back in New York.

The buzz of New York that winter caught Jimmy's imagination. He revisited the Actors' Studio, sitting in on workshops, indulged his photographic passion, played his bongo drums at various clubs and began to study new dance techniques at a class also attended by Eartha Kitt. In September, before he left Hollywood, he had begun discussing a new film project with director Nicholas Ray, and the talks continued in New York.

After Warner Brothers' announcement that Jimmy was to star in Ray's new film, *Rebel Without a Cause*, Jimmy returned to California on 18 January 1955 for more talks. Unable to settle into the new work, he became increasingly agitated as *Eden*'s public première approached. This was held on 9 March 1955 at New York's Astor Theatre. A gala evening in the best Hollywood tradition, its proceeds were to go towards the Actors' Studio. Both Marilyn Monroe and Marlene Dietrich acted as guest usherettes.

Jimmy tried to avoid the ballyhoo by arriving nearly four hours late for the pre-screening press conference. Immediately afterwards he took flight back to California and Nick Ray's film. Jane Deacy was left to placate Warner Brothers. The première went ahead as planned and attracted the largest-ever-recorded crowds in Times Square, with notices in the New York press confirming the arrival of a new star on the Hollywood horizon. His future seemed assured. It would be the only film of Dean's career that he would live to see released.

3
Rebel Without a Cause

'Boy, if I had one day when I didn't have to be all confused and didn't have to feel that I was ashamed of everything.'

Jim Stark in *Rebel Without a Cause*, 1955

A few pages of Nick Ray's shooting script were enough to convince Jane Deacy that the role of Jim Stark in *Rebel Without a Cause* was tailor-made for Jimmy.

Based on a true-life study of a psychopathic teenager documented by Dr Robert Linder, *The Blind Run* had been Warner Brothers' property since 1946, but it had been shelved as unsuitable for movie audiences in the late 'forties. However, with the upheaval caused by rock and roll, and the advent of movies like MGM's *The Blackboard Jungle* in the 'fifties, the time now seemed ripe to dust off the story.

Ever-cautious, Warner Brothers had planned the film as a low-budget vehicle to be shot in black and white, economizing on both cast and locations. However, Nick Ray's realization of the story and the performances of his hand-picked actors in early rushes persuaded the studio to raise the investment and re-shoot in Cinemascope. The sudden injection of colour made cinematic history at Warner Brothers' wardrobe department, which had the task of distressing 400 pairs of Levis to give the right effect on colour film.

Faced with a re-shoot of the infamous knife-fight sequence outside the observatory, Jimmy suggested that Ray dispense with the stand-ins, and that he and Corey Allen (Buzz) should do the scene themselves, wearing protective vests and using real flick-knives. Ray agreed, and Jimmy was able to use much of his recently acquired dance technique in the scene, which he choreographed like a ballet. Considered an incitement to teenage violence, the re-filmed sequence was severely cut on the initial release of *Rebel* in 1956.

That Jimmy could suggest and be taken up on ideas by his director reflected a unique working relationship, very different from Kazan's pseudo-parental stance. From their first meeting, Nick Ray and Jimmy had developed a strong kindred spirit. On the rebound from Kazan, Jimmy needed a father figure to identify with, and Ray filled this role.

During their meetings in New York in the winter of 1954, Ray had suggested improvising around the script – such as it was – rather than adhering to it word for word. From that moment a bond was forged and Jimmy spent much of his time re-working the script with Ray.

When he did escape from the studio it was to drive his new 1500cc Porsche Speedster with the garage mechanic Rolf Weutherich. Jimmy had found a loophole in Warner Brothers' no-racing clause: it related only to motorbikes. Before the company realized what was happening, Jimmy had notched up six outright victories at racetrack events and found himself accepted by the racing fraternity.

The first day's filming of *Rebel Without a Cause* was 28 March 1955. In this film, Jimmy offered a greater insight to his personality than anywhere else on celluloid and it soon became apparent that Jimmy wasn't acting the role of Jim Stark – he *was* Jim Stark. Day by day the film was becoming increasingly autobiographical. What Jimmy had been unable to face at Strasberg's critical analysis at the Actors' Studio, and had found unrewarding at the analyst's sessions, he was able to confess to the camera without hesitation.

Like *East of Eden*, the film, which covers a 24-hour period, deals with a strained father-and-son relationship. From the pre-credit sequence to the final curtain-down, Jimmy is always present, as one of three out-of-joint adolescents who, as the film opens, have been rounded up by the police. Jim Stark is struggling to understand why his father (Jim Backus) has no authority in the female-dominated family and fails to lend his son moral support; the school loner, Plato (Sal Mineo), cannot cope with his friendless, broken-home existence and seeks security in a gun; Judy (Natalie Wood), once 'daddy's little girl', cannot comprehend why her father should increasingly reject her natural affection. Stark, beginning yet another new school, fails to win friends by his antics, and is soon made the butt of the school gang, egged on into a knife-fight with the gang's leader and Judy's boyfriend, Buzz (Corey Allen). Their clash is to be resolved in a 'chicken run' later that night. Using two stolen cars, each driver races towards a cliff edge, the first to jump free being labelled 'chicken'. Buzz is trapped in his car, fails to escape and goes over the bluff with his car. Stark's instinct is to face the music and inform the police, but his parents wish to avoid trouble. The other gang members sense his intentions and pursue Jimmy and Judy, now fellow sufferers and as a consequence lovers, to a hideout provided by Plato – an old mansion on the edge of town. There they act out their fantasies by pretending to be house-hunting newly-weds. The gang catches up with the trio but is frightened away by Plato's gun and the arrival of the police. Stark tries to shield Plato but he is shot dead by a policeman after

Stark has already unloaded the pistol and persuaded Plato to surrender.

Unlike Kazan, who firmly controlled his actors, Nick Ray allowed Jimmy to build up his character as he saw it and readily acknowledged him as co-director of the movie. Jimmy's freedom to improvise allowed him to indulge in the most private self-expression, and at times it was as if he was documenting his own life-story. The location used for the fictional Dawson High School was the Santa Monica Community College, where five years earlier Jimmy had dropped out of his pre-law course to enrol at UCLA. By May they were filming the night scenes at Griffith Park, Los Angeles, where Jimmy had made the Pepsi-Cola commercial.

A tight shooting schedule gave Jimmy little time to surface and leave the film and his character behind. Warner Brothers pressed Jimmy into a pre-production lunch conference on 18 May for *Giant*, having announced in April that he would play Jett Rink. Following a full evening's filming, Jimmy arrived dressed in jeans and T-shirt, unshaven and wearing dark glasses. This did not meet with Warner's approval, and his refusal to pose for the press photographer or talk to columnists immediately soured his relations with the production team, particularly the director, George Stevens. Jimmy also snubbed Elizabeth Taylor, though more from nerves than by premeditation. These unintentional expressions of disenchantment would increase later in the year when filming began.

For the present, Jimmy used his rare moments of spare time trying to telephone Brando and Clift, seeking their advice and, with child-like innocence, wishing to share his movie-making experiences with them. But the messages remained unanswered on their answering machines. Jimmy steered clear of the studio's big names, Tracy, Bogart and Gable, but found some affinity with Gary Cooper, who visited the set several times and invited Jimmy to his home for dinner. The formal side of Hollywood had never attracted Jimmy, however, and he felt more at ease with fellow *Rebel* actor Jack Simmons (Moose) and the TV personality Maila Nurmi, who hosted a chat show under the pseudonym of 'Vampira'. The three would often talk over the day's events late at night.

Jimmy's working days, some of them amounting to screened confessions, were intensive and emotionally draining. Yet they were therapeutic. Jane Deacy, realizing this, managed to slip Jimmy into a television playlet at CBS. *The Unlighted Road*, in which he again played a disturbed teenager, was Dean's last television play.

The filming of *Rebel Without a Cause* ended on 25 May 1955 at a cost of only $600,000. It was the end of a mutually creative partnership, on which both Jimmy and Ray intended to build. (Even at this stage in his career, Jimmy was developing ambitions to write and direct his own productions.) This time Jimmy had no time to sink into depression. Taking leave of Nick Ray was limited to a brief farewell tour of the sound stages. Both instinctively knew that something special had been created and captured on film.

Rebel Without a Cause opened at New York's Astor Theatre on 26 October 1955, one month after the death of its star.

4

Giant

*'Ain't nobody king in this country. Ain't nobody,
no matter what they might be thinking.'*

Jett Rink in *Giant*, 1956

Preliminary shooting of *Giant* had already begun earlier in May, before *Rebel Without a Cause* was finished, but Jimmy was not required until 3 June, when the unit would move from Charlottesville, Virginia, to Texas, and he took advantage of the situation by racing in a weekend meet on 28 and 29 May in his Porsche Speedster at Santa Barbara.

Giant was a major undertaking for Warner Brothers. Its gestation period had been long, matching the painstaking pace of its director George Stevens. Stevens had begun translating Edna Ferber's 477-page novel into a shooting script while Jimmy was filming *East of Eden*. *Giant* was to cost an estimated $5 million (it grossed $7 million in its first year alone).

Initial contenders for the major role of the farmhand, Jett Rink, who strikes oil, had included Alan Ladd (fresh from Stevens' *Shane*) and Richard Burton. Soon after Jimmy's contract with Warner Brothers had been extended, Jane Deacy had successfully convinced a reluctant Stevens that Jimmy was right for the part: his performance in *East of Eden* was the only argument she needed. The big box-office draws Elizabeth Taylor and Rock Hudson would receive top billing; Jimmy would not hold centre stage this time, although his characterization of Rink was central to the story-line.

Giant related the grand, sweeping story of the Benedict family over a period of some 30 years spent at Reata, their half-a-million-acre ranch in Texas. Luz Benedict (Mercedes McCambridge) has the upper hand over her brother Bick (Rock Hudson) in the running of the ranch, and is not pleased when he returns from a horse-buying trip with a bride, Lesley Lynton (Elizabeth Taylor). Jett Rink (James Dean) is one of Reata's cowhands, much disliked by Bick. When Luz is killed riding the horse Bick brought back with his new wife, Rink inherits a few acres of land from her, much to the annoyance of Bick, who tries without success to buy it from Rink. Rink baptises his small-holding Little Reata, works the land alone, and is lucky enough to strike oil. Unable to contain his delight, Rink immediately bursts in on the Benedicts, smothered in the black oil. As Rink's wealth increases he becomes a ruthless oil baron, and the hatred between him and Bick intensifies. The years go by and Bick and Lesley's children marry and have children in their turn; the cattle ranch has to surrender to the might of the oil field; and Rink becomes ever richer, taking over towns, hospitals and airports. It is at the opening of his latest hotel that the final confrontation between Rink and Bick takes place, provoked by the beating up of the Benedicts' son Jordan (Dennis Hopper) by Rink's heavies. In the hotel's vast wine store an inebriated Rink is beaten up in a fist-fight by Bick. The Benedicts depart for Reata, leaving the wine-soaked and incoherent Rink now slumped across the head table to address a deserted banqueting hall.

Giant was already fifteen days into production when Jimmy joined the unit for an arduous four weeks' filming in the Texas backwater town of Marfa, where he found himself sharing a home with Rock Hudson. The filming was by no means as rewarding an experience as it had been with either Kazan or Ray. Stevens came from an older school of film-making and did not encourage long discussions with his actors. He was unhappy about Jimmy's unpredictable behaviour during rehearsals and the actor's continual experimentation with the script inevitably gave rise to mistakes that Stevens found difficult to stomach. Moreover, the preparation time Jimmy needed for a scene contributed to a tense irritability between director and actor, which built up as the film progressed. Soon Jimmy's quarrels with Stevens spilled over into his relations with the rest of his colleagues. Dennis Hopper, Sal Mineo and Elizabeth Taylor were the only actors who were on good terms with him.

At 23 and just married to Michael Wilding, Elizabeth Taylor was the undisputed Queen of Hollywood. On their first take together, feeling insufficiently at ease to enter into his scene with her, Jimmy left the set and urinated in front of the massed on-lookers to help him control his nerves. Hopper and Mineo, who had been in *Rebel Without a Cause* and followed Jimmy into *Giant*, were used to his antics, but this and similar behaviour did not endear him to those who did not know and understand him.

A new friend was the stills photographer employed on *Giant*, Sanford Roth, with whom Jimmy had long discussions during the tedious interludes while scenes not involving him were being shot.

After location shooting everyone moved back to the studios for the interior work, but this only increased the strain between Jimmy and Stevens. Most of Jimmy's scenes had been filmed out in Marfa, and he had fewer appearances in the studio sessions. For the irritable young actor, waiting around in make-up from early morning on the off-chance that they might shoot a scene with him was hard to take. The team involvement of working with Ray was missing and he had long since lost interest in the project.

He worked out a system whereby one of the crew was to sneak him details of when he would be needed on the studio floor, so that he could stay away from the studio when he was not needed. In August he had taken out a one-year lease on a house in the San Fernando Valley at Sherman Oaks, and so he took off there to wait for his cues. When Mercedes McCambridge was taken ill and Stevens changed his routine, Jimmy was found out and Elizabeth Taylor drove over to Sherman Oaks to bring him back to the studio. Stevens took the situation as a personal insult and severely reprimanded Jimmy in front of the entire shooting crew. This nearly spelled the end of Jimmy's involvement in the picture.

As in *East of Eden*, Jimmy ceased to differentiate between his on- and off-screen personae. Stevens became the stand-in for Raymond Massey's disapproving father in *East of Eden*, who in turn had been a stand-in for Jimmy's real father, Winton Dean. Jimmy's rebellion against a father figure who neither accepted nor understood him formed a sharp contrast to his positive working relationship with Nick Ray during *Rebel Without a Cause*. Jimmy's feeling of antagonism spread through the entire *Giant* crew, and the atmosphere was fraught.

Jimmy turned to his new friends, the Roths, and sought out another new Hollywood starlet, the Swiss daughter of the German Consul in Berne – Ursula Andress. A brief affair followed, but Andress eventually dropped Jimmy for the actor John Derek. Unlike Pier Angeli, Andress would not accept Jimmy's eccentricities. He was his own worst enemy and could not see that his behaviour had already driven away Bill Bast and Leonard Rosenman, and had been instrumental in the ending of his affair with Angeli.

Rejected once more, he tried working out his frustrations in sculpting lessons from Pegot Waring, biding his time until the close of the film. His only confidante outside the studio was Maila Nurmi, whom he regularly met at the Sunset Boulevard hang-out 'Googie's'.

His house in San Fernando saw few visitors. His only companion was a Siamese cat, a present from Elizabeth Taylor, christened Young Marcus after his Fairmount cousin.

While shooting the final scenes on *Giant*, he was asked to help out the National Highway Committee by taking part in a television commercial. He agreed, and, interviewed by fellow actor Gig Young, spoke of his racing achievements while toying with a lariat. He concluded with a prophetic warning against reckless driving: 'Remember, drive safely because the life you save may be mine.'

Jane Deacy came out to discuss a new Warner Brothers contract. He was to be guaranteed $1 million over the next six years, with three months off each year to spend as he wished. Jimmy's new wealth allowed him to indulge his racing passion, and he traded in his Porsche Speedster for a Porsche Spyder 550. He asked the artist George Barris to customize the silver aluminium car with the racing number 130 on the bonnet and doors, and with its nickname of 'the little bastard'. He also ordered two English cars, a Lotus 8 and a more powerful Bristol, with a view to bigger track events.

On 22 September, *Giant* was concluded as the 'last supper' banquet scenes were wrapped up. A special preview of these rushes was held five days later before a guest audience, but characteristically Jimmy arrived at the viewing theatre as the lights were going up after the showing. The night drew the final curtain over Jimmy's part in *Giant*. Having finished filming, Stevens saw little reason for his unco-operative star to stay on. As if by mutual agreement, there were no goodbyes.

Keen to get away from Warner Brothers for a spell, and having heard of a weekend racing event in Salinas, Jimmy phoned up and booked himself into the race.

It would be more than a year before *Giant* was released, winning Stevens an Oscar for Best Director and acting nominations for both Jimmy and Rock Hudson.

5
The Legend

'That guy up there has got to stop. He's seen us.'
James Dean, 30 September 1955

O n paper at least the last weeks of September 1955 seemed
full of promise for Jimmy. Deacy's re-negotiations with Warner
Brothers had been successful. Jimmy had financial security and
was already ear-marked for the role of the New York boxer Rocky
Graziano in a biopic to be made at MGM (part repayment for the loan
of Elizabeth Taylor in *Giant*). Also under discussion was the part of
Billy the Kid in *The Left-Handed Gun*. Ironically, both parts went to
Paul Newman after Jimmy's death. Jimmy told Deacy that he would
like to use some of his money on a visit to Europe, to prepare for a
return to the New York stage as Hamlet. More immediate was the
forthcoming NBC TV special of Emlyn Williams' *The Corn Is Green*,
for the extraordinary fee of $20,000.

Now that he was a man of substance, Deacy persuaded Jimmy to
make a will. Jimmy arranged to visit a lawyer after his return from the
Salinas meeting. In the meantime, he took out a life insurance policy
with Lew Bracker, Leonard Rosenman's nephew, nominating his
Fairmount 'family' as beneficiaries. (On Jimmy's death Winton Dean
inherited his entire estate since no will was ever drawn up.)

After Warner Brothers' ban on racing during filming, Jimmy was
bubbling at the idea of the forthcoming race meeting. Time was short.
He needed to run in the Spyder's engine and Rolf Weutherich, now
his 'official' pit-stop mechanic, needed to re-adjust it before the race
at Salinas. By Thursday, the Spyder's speedometer registered only
about 100 miles, so Jimmy suggested driving up to Salinas, weather

permitting, instead of loading the car on to the station wagon's trailer.

In festive spirit Jimmy tried to entice everyone to join him in Salinas. His return to the track was an occasion to celebrate and Jimmy wanted to share his enthusiasm with friends. But his aunt and uncle were returning to Fairmount; Nick Ray had gone to London; Nick Adams and Richard Davalos were leaving for a play in New York. In the end the party consisted of Rolf Weutherich, Sanford Roth, who was keen to get some photographs of Jimmy, and *Giant* stuntman and racing fanatic Bill Hickman. Roth and Hickman would take the Ford station wagon and Jimmy and Weutherich would travel in the open-topped Spyder.

The day, 30 September, proved perfect for the trip, with warm and sunny weather. The band of four set off in the early afternoon on Highway 99, heading north from Los Angeles. Jimmy was dressed in his usual gear of jeans, white T-shirt and red nylon blouson. Just outside Bakersfield they were flagged down by a traffic cop and given speeding tickets for doing 70 mph in a 45-mph zone.

Jimmy soon lost Roth and Hickman in the station wagon, and pulled in at Blackwells Corner on Route 46 to stretch his legs and check out a new Mercedes 300SL he had spotted. Waiting for the others, Jimmy discovered that the owner, Lance Reventlow, Barbara Hutton's son and heir to the Woolworth fortune, was also heading for the meet. Growing impatient, Jimmy clambered back into 'the little bastard' and took off.

The countryside grew more arid as the sun began to set. The two friends fell silent and Jimmy nudged the car up to 100 mph, eager to reach Paso Robles, while Weutherich dozed. As they approached the small town of Cholame at about 5.45 p.m, a black and white Ford sedan, driven by a 23-year-old student, Donald Turnupseed, travelling south-east on the 466, drew across the junction with Highway 41 blocking Jimmy's path. When he spotted the sedan Jimmy dropped his speed and exclaimed, 'That guy's gotta stop'.

As the Ford continued across the highway, Jimmy braked and went into a skid. The lightweight car flew off the road and crumpled like paper against a telegraph pole. Jimmy was impaled on the steering column, his head flung back at the impact of the crash with such force that it broke his neck. Turnupseed had been thrown into the windscreen of the Ford, badly cutting his face. Weutherich lay unconscious on the verge, with broken limbs and a fractured jaw. Jimmy had died within seconds of impact.

Roth and Hickman drew up about ten minutes later at the gathering of passing motorists who had stopped to help. A patrol car and an ambulance had been called. Roth found himself taking photographs in case they might be needed as evidence, while Hickman tried to comfort Weutherich. The ambulance crew took seven minutes to extricate Jimmy's body from the carnage, and, with Weutherich, they drove back to Paso Robles War Memorial Hospital. Later that night Jimmy's corpse was identified in the morgue by Winton Dean.

During the evening the news of Jimmy's death began filtering through Hollywood. The following morning it made headlines in all media. On 4 October, the body was flown back to Indiana accompanied by Winton Dean. It lay for three days at Hunt's Funeral Parlour in Fairmount, where, a year before, showing off, Jimmy had posed in an empty coffin for a *Life* photographer.

The funeral service took place on 8 October at 2 p.m. at the Friends' Back Creek Church, drawing a congregation that outnumbered the town's population. The service was conducted by Jimmy's one-time mentor, the Rev. James De-Weerd, and he was buried just north of Fairmount in the Park Cemetery. Among those at the graveside were *Giant* producer Henry Ginsberg and *Rebel* scriptwriter Stewart Stern. The coffin was carried by six of Jimmy's former high school friends. In Paso Robles, a coroner's jury listened to the details of the accident as it was recreated and after twenty minutes delivered a verdict of accidental death. No charges were brought against Turnupseed, and controversy was rife.

Warner Brothers were cautious in their response to Jimmy's death. The films of Jean Harlow and Carol Lombard had been box-office failures after the deaths of their stars, and Jack Warner believed that nobody would pay to see a corpse. As a result, the October première of *Rebel Without a Cause* was initially cancelled, and even the press book at the première of *Giant* in October the following year gave no real indication that the actor playing Jett Rink had died. However, Warner Brothers need not have worried. Jimmy's death drew a following unequalled in Hollywood since the passing of Valentino. In many ways it was only the beginning

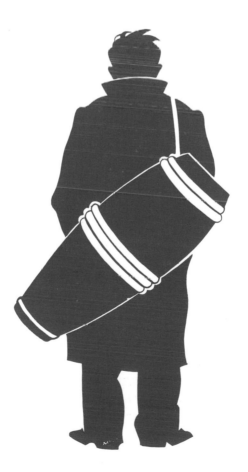

Reflections

He is like a chrysalis baby folded out of its cocoon. Turned in on himself. A solitude that is suffered rather than willed, a tortured quest for affection, for love or friendship.

ERIC ROHMER

He was a hero to the people who saw him as a waif, when actually he was a pudding of hatred.

ELIA KAZAN

In James Dean, today's youth discovers itself. Less for the reasons usually advanced — violence, sadism, hysteria, pessimism, cruelty and filth — than for others infinitely more simple and commonplace: modesty of feeling, continual fantasy life, moral purity without relation to everyday morality but all the more rigorous, eternal adolescent love of tests and trials, intoxication, pride and regret at feeling 'outside' society, refusal and desire to become integrated and, finally, acceptance — or refusal — of the world as it is.

FRANÇOIS TRUFFAUT

Jim was an unusual student and friend. We kept in touch through the years following his graduation from Fairmount High. His power of concentration was tremendous, and anything he set his mind to do, he did with his whole heart. I am grateful to have had a genius in my classroom.

ADELINE MART NALL

Dean's potency was not that of a rebel without a cause. Although he was vulnerable and sensitive, he never suggested youthfulness or callowness. On the contrary, he seemed older, sadder and more experienced than the adults in his films. More than that, he seemed to sense his own extra intuition and to see that it was of no use. His resignation and fatalism showed up the restricted personality of the world he inhabited. Occasionally driven to anger or violence, Dean was not a rebel, but a disenchanted romantic, as brooding and knowing as the darkest Bogart. He appealed to the young because he understood that youth knew some truths about the world that adults had looked away from: about the unfriendly cities, the instinct for violence and forsaken emotional sensibility.

DAVID THOMSON

A tough kid who sleeps on nails.

HOWARD SACKLER

James Dean was great in two respects – he had great timing and great hair. Essentially that is what made him a hero of youth culture. I suspect he was also a good actor – but that is another matter altogether.

RAY CONNOLLY

James Dean on the screen was exactly what every kid on the block wanted to be. I'm sure the old movies and clips of Dean on film will still be watched for generations to come.

ROBIN COUSINS

Everything was perfect. The face, the smile, the movements of the head, the movements of the body – and the accent, the charm, the voice.

LESLIE CARON

Dean represented the defeated teenager: sensitive, incoherent, rebellious, moody, grave, the victim of adult misunderstanding. What's more, his early death secured him instant and comparatively permanent beatification. I went to see one of his films the other day and a large section of the audience were young enough to have been children when it was first released. Yet the atmosphere was reverent, almost church-like. Death is the one certain way to preserve a pop legend, because age, itself, is considered a compromise.

GEORGE MELLY

That man knew where it was at, he was rocking.

MICK JAGGER

40

East of Eden displayed a remarkable welding of actor to role, or vice versa, that was responsible for Dean's elevation from rebellious Broadway actor to spokesman for the 'generation gap' youth of his era. To them Dean was far more than an actor: he was a symbol of a generation which no longer had anything in common with its parents. Always at loggerheads with authority, Dean's personality was the essence of an age characterized by youthful rebellion, and he was worshipped as such.

CLIVE HIRSCHHORN

He was desperately lonely and had many inward problems, so it was hard to get close to him. He was a strange and sensitive character with tremendous imagination.

JULIE HARRIS

Dean had an astonishing hold on the adolescent imagination; he brought authority to the role of the 'crazy-mixed-up kid'.

JOE MORELLA

I have great respect for his talent. However, in East of Eden, Mr Dean appears to be wearing my last year's wardrobe and using my last year's talent. Just a lost boy trying to find himself.

MARLON BRANDO

One felt that he was a boy one had to take care of, but even that was probably his joke. I don't think he needed anybody or anything – except his acting.

ELIZABETH TAYLOR

He didn't comb his hair. He had a safety-pin holding his pants together. He was introspective and very shy. When he landed at LA, Jimmy looked like a 'dead-beat' straight from the Bronx, complete with a parcel tied with string under his arm containing all his belongings.

ELIA KAZAN

JAMES DEAN

His acting goes against 50 years of film-making. Each gesture, each attitude, each mime is a slap in the face of tradition. James Dean's acting is more animal than human. That is what makes it unpredictable. He can begin to turn his back to the camera whilst speaking, throw his head back or roll it forwards, he can raise his arms or push them forward. I le belongs to those who pay no heed to rules and laws.

MARCEAU DEVILLERS

His method mannerisms may long since have lost their novelty, as have Brando's: but these mannerisms, like Brando's, were always just the top-dressing of his histrionic talent; beneath them lay a virtuosity of cinematic nuances and timing, together with an authentic ability to communicate the heights and depths and subtleties of a wide range of feelings.

DOUGLAS McVAY

Everyone got the idea it was a sloppy, don't-give-a-damn kind of group. This is not so. To begin with, Dean was scarcely at the Studio at all. He came in a few times and slouched in the front row. He never participated in anything.

LEE STRASBERG

7he Dean visual was also an important milestone in gay imagery. During the early, struggling stages of his career, Dean actively cultivated the clean-cut, blond, brush-cut athlete look that was such a major theme in the gay pin-ups of the period immediately following World War II. It was a quality that Dean never quite lost even at the height of his brooding prime. As a gay sex symbol he was the link between the Tab Hunter, shower-scene jocks and the new, mysterious, black-jacketed kids who were studying to look like Elvis Presley. It's more than possible that Dean's image planted some of the first seeds that would, over the next two decades, blossom into the leather-men in their straps and caps and handlebar moustaches that are a regulation sub-group on every gay cruising strip in the Western World.

MICK FARREN

*C*reating a personal image or look is probably one of the most difficult things to achieve without being over the top. With James Dean it came naturally, along with Marilyn Monroe and Clark Gable. The latter two have been cloned by a few, but ironically if James Dean had still been alive he would have found a reflection of himself in the typical male youth of today. His image lives once again.

TOMMY NUTTER

*A*s fine an actor as James Dean was, I did not find him enigmatic or inspiring. One always felt his own personality intruded upon his performances.

BILL GIBB

He was pure gold. The images he created on screen in his three films are as contemporary today as they were when they were made. He was one of the greatest actors that ever lived.

DENNIS HOPPER

He's not an idol of mine, and I didn't particularly like what he was.

ELIA KAZAN

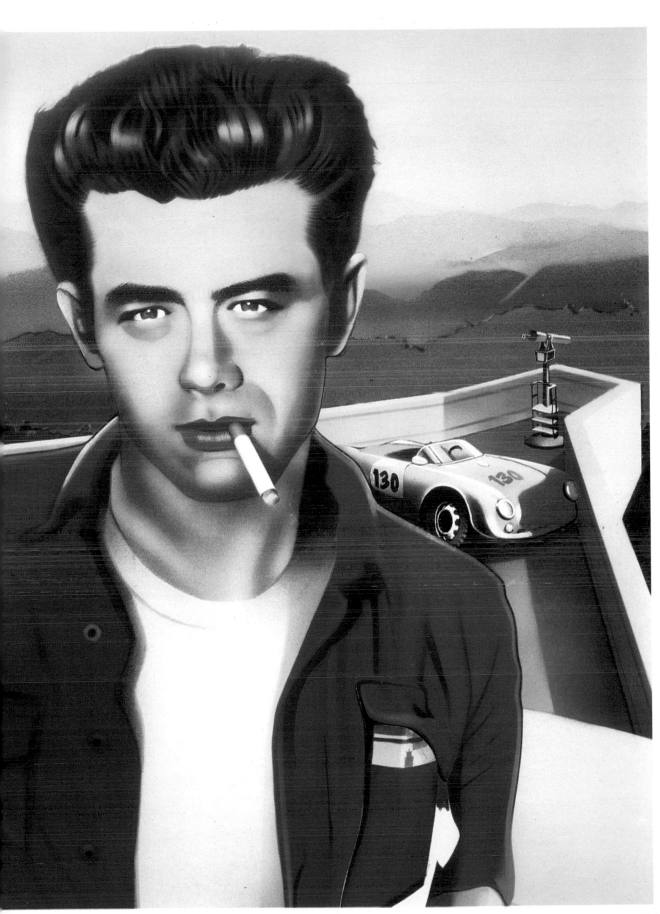

*J*ames Dean was sentenced by physique to stand for defencelessness, and some instinct, far more than the actor's technique, taught him how to suggest, behind the mask of rebelliousness, a different being – shrinking, fragile, not quite fully grown.

DILYS POWELL

Jimmy was all art – 'always on', says Roy Schatt – always acting. The James Dean who had himself introduced to me wanted something and he was out to let me see what he looked like without glasses, which he needed badly. He knew that he had Brando for competition. When I opened the doors to the studio – a room full of Steve Reeves! So he was not only up against our greatest actor, but the most beautiful guy in the world! What trick, what strategy would he use to wean me away from these giants in their class? He would save it for the last second. We talked and agreed. He stepped outside the door, put out his hand, positioning himself into an almost-bow, and looked up into my eyes opening his mouth into a smile he threw the whole personality at me. He had turned himself into the most beautiful thing God ever created. It was like being struck by lightning. That kid knew what he was doing! If James Dean walked into your life things would never be the same. That's as close as we're ever going to get to seeing an enchanted prince – but then it wouldn't surprise me if he were the Angel of Death.

KENNETH KENDALL

I realized that I was dealing with a talent that was pure gold. I said to him, 'Jimmy, people will be watching that long after we've gone and they'll still think it's great.' This seemed to please him tremendously.

ELIA KAZAN

Sometimes Jimmy wouldn't even hear you when you spoke to him, he would just switch off . . . but he was always polite and nice to be with. At that time a lot of people were snubbing him. Maybe they were frightened of this startling new talent that was so completely different from anything we knew at that time. If those people think their pools or their Cadillacs are threatened, they pull up the drawbridge – and quickly. I often wonder, if he had lived, what sort of movies he'd be making now. You can bet they'd be first-class entertainment. That's the business we're in, and Jimmy knew that better than most.

NATALIE WOOD

Anyone who came into contact with Jimmy found that their lives were never quite the same again. God knows where a spirit like that comes from. They flash across our lives like shooting stars.

ELIZABETH TAYLOR

You couldn't take your eyes off him, but you weren't sure you ever wanted to see him again.

GARY CAREY

James Dean did live fast and he did die young, and he was a brilliant actor, but these factors alone were no guarantee of cinematic immortality. What finally did it for him was good timing. He was exactly the right image, and displayed precisely the right attitude for teenagers growing up in the mid-'fifties, and, in the end, he came to represent far more than either the sum total of his looks or his talent. He came to represent, in fact, not just his own generation of young people, but every young person who ever quarrelled with his parents or challenged authority.

TERENCE PETTIGREW

I taught Jimmy to believe in personal immortality. He had no fear of death because he believed that death is merely control of mind over matter.

Dr JAMES DE-WEERD

On screen he is every adolescent fear and fantasy incarnate. Every step he takes on screen is a metaphor for your wildest dreams and darkest moments: he defines and defends you, he is the Peter Pan of pop culture posing the question, 'When are you going to grow up?'

TONY PARSONS

This image of Dean as the archetypal victim of an unbridgeable generation gap had begun with East of Eden. He was so right and true as Cal that spectators accustomed to accepting the actor as the character were instinctive in their response. Dean brought it closer, because he acted better. Cal, in elation when his crops are doing well; in compulsive violence and love-making; in resentment and even in spite, was the forerunner of the modern misfit of Rebel Without a Cause, whose conflict with his parents served to emphasize the identification point for youth of the 'fifties. A social demarcation between his middle-class rebel and the arrogant hoodlum played by Brando in The Wild One was not sufficient in itself to obliterate the similarity between Dean and Brando. Unalike in appearance, they nevertheless had much the same mode of speech, and to a certain degree the same manner of deportment, befitting the characters they played.

GORDON GOW

He was very protective of himself. He was a very sensitive guy. My feeling is that he didn't really allow people into him because he was very busy protecting his awareness that he had. He didn't want to be split up socially and to find himself playing games, and so he stayed with himself. When he felt very secure then occasionally he would open up.

COREY ALLEN

Jimmy would swear — I remember he'd say 'fuck' or something like that — and Raymond Massey would turn scarlet and finally had to say once: 'You musn't talk like that. There are ladies present,' which just egged Jimmy on more.

JULIE HARRIS

In every respect he was the Cal of Steinbeck's novel. He was to become a sort of cult with the young. Jimmy had only to act himself. But that is a difficult role even for an experienced actor to play. A rebel at heart, he approached everything with a chip on his shoulder. Jimmy never knew his lines before he walked on the set, rarely had command of them when the camera rolled and even if he had was often inaudible. Simple technicalities, such as moving on cue and finding his marks, were beneath his consideration. Equally annoying was his insistence on going away alone once a scene was rehearsed and everything ready for a take. He would disappear and leave the rest to cool off in our chairs while he communed with himself somewhere out of sight. When he was ready we would hear the whistle Gadge Kazan had given given him and he would reappear. We would assemble to our appointed spots and the camera would roll.

You know and we all know that Jimmy's got it. He's good. But there are rules to go by in our profession and he'd better abide by them. One is to stick to the script.

RAYMOND MASSEY

I remember the last day of filming. It was terrible for me. You always feel that you're alone in these feelings, whatever you feel. You feel that nobody else can possibly feel that. The last scene was shot – I don't know what scene we were working on. It was the exterior of the house, I know that. And there was to be a party that night. It was awful for me that last day to think that it had all gone away, that life we'd been leading for two-and-a-half months. You wouldn't see anybody again. You wouldn't come there every day. You wouldn't look forward to it. And I remember looking around and thinking, I've got to say goodbye to Jimmy. And suddenly, all the set was just deserted, and everybody had gone. And he had a dressing room, on the set, and I went up to the caravan and knocked on the door and I thought I heard something like a sob. I said, 'Jimmy', and then knocked again. So then I was sure it was a sob and I opened the door and he was just in tears, his eyes and I said 'What's the matter?', and he said, 'It's over, it's over', and he was like a little boy. So lovely.

JULIE HARRIS

James Dean never consciously sought to be a god, or indeed, a symbol for anything. He wanted to be a star, and he wanted to enjoy the limelight, but the idea of heading a huge tidal wave of teenage revolt against the narrow, repressive, adult double-speak of the mid-'fifties did not occur to him.

TERENCE PETTIGREW

He was very aware of the fact that he was a star. There was no escaping it. I mean, eyes were on him. I remember when we did a television show before we did Rebel, *we used to go to lunch on his motorcycle to a nearby hamburger joint. He used to be fascinated by the stories that were being written about him in the movie magazines, you know. There was a lot of them about his love affair with Pier Angeli, and he would read them. He wouldn't buy them, but he would be fascinated. . . . And then he'd throw them.*

NATALIE WOOD

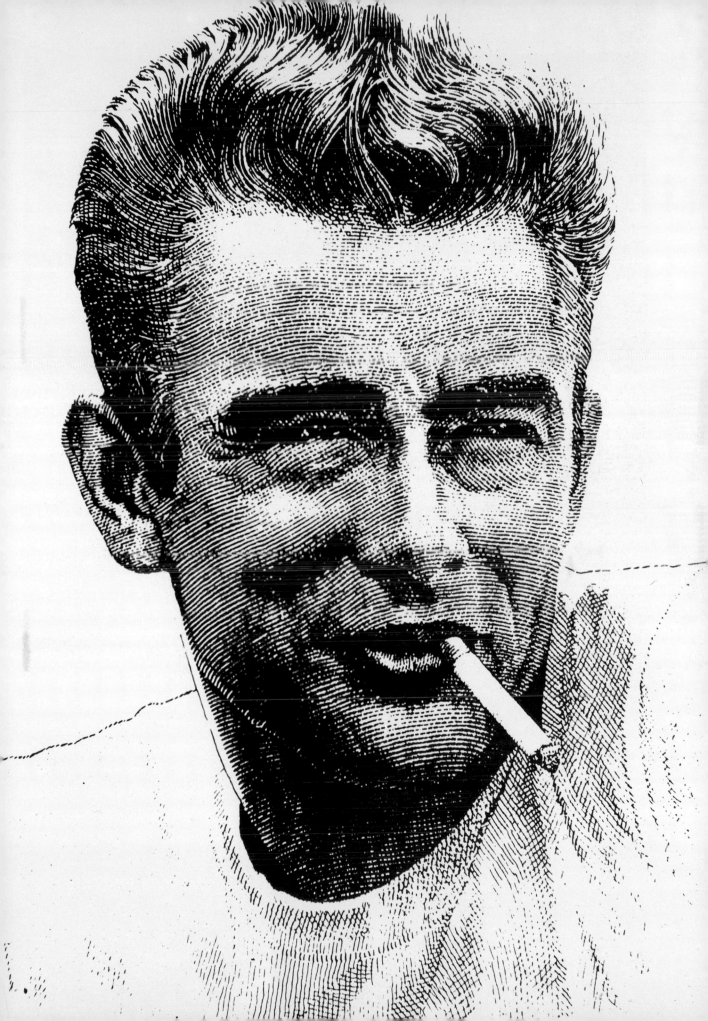

ames Dean gave a name and a style to a generation. He was the original 'mixed-up kid'. When he said in his second, provocatively titled film Rebel Without a Cause, *'How can a guy grow up in a circus like this?' he struck a familiar chord with teenagers everywhere who felt out of sorts with parents that, unlike Andy Hardy's, could no longer hand down the verdict on life in ways that would be obeyed around the family dinner table. Dean spoke romantically for the 'hurt' children of post-war upheaval. His face had the flickering, mobile uncertainties of adolescence continually passing over it; his speech was a secret mumble; his short-sightedness gave him a naturally withdrawn look; and he put his resistance to adult convention into the purposeful sloppiness of his dress. Even the way he walked had the attitude of the loner – hunched up, not 'switched on', like someone whose youthful enthusiasm has been killed by some secret shock to his system. He set the style – and premature death established the myth that achieved a morbid fulfilment in the last three years of the 1950s, when he became one of the first superstars whose posthumous image was sedulously and profitably fostered by commercial merchandising.*

ALEXANDER WALKER

For the first time in the history of mankind the teenager was liberated. After seeing Rebel Without a Cause *I went out and bought a red windcheater, and so did thousands of others.*

ADAM FAITH

I know by heart all the dialogue of James Dean's films. I could watch Rebel *a hundred times over.*

ELVIS PRESLEY

I didn't pick Jimmy for Rebel, we sniffed each other out, like a couple of Siamese cats. We went to New York together so I could see where he lived. You should have seen his room – a tiny place, cluttered with books and boxes.

NICK RAY

CINEMABILIA

Narcissistic, self-centred, arrogant, often witty, yet at the same time vulnerable and sad, James Dean struck a familiar chord with millions of young people — and troubled their elders. He was no flatterer, didn't make friends easily, but could be thoughtful, considerate and attentive.

ROGER ST PIERRE

I always had the feeling there was in Jimmy a sort of doomed quality.

LEE STRASBERG

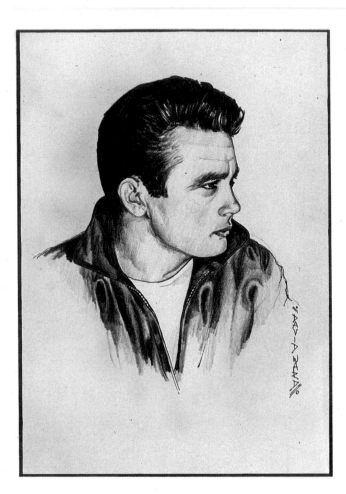

To his generation, and for all film historians, Dean will always represent the ultimate rebel, the symbol of self-pitying youth, rebelling against the insecurity and loneliness in his own soul.

JOE MORELLA

From what I'd seen of Jimmy on the set I didn't know what the fuss was about. Then I saw the screening, and you know, he was great. He was sitting just behind me in the cinema and a half-a-dozen times, when he was really terrific, I turned round to look at him. He was giving that grin of his and almost blushing, looking down at the floor between his legs.

SAL MINEO

Even today at odd times I find myself thinking of Jimmy and how much he helped us all. He often comes in to my mind that way. A while back I was out West filming, so I took a look around the Rebel location. The tears just flowed . . . I had to get away fast.

SAL MINEO

I think that really he was not a rebel, in the sense that he was not rejecting parents. He wasn't saying, 'Leave me alone. I don't want to have anything to do with you. I'm going to do my own thing.' He was really saying, 'Listen to me, hear me, love me.'

NATALIE WOOD

*I*ntense and moody in contrast to the surfers and beach bunnies, with unruly looks and wearing the same blue jacket and grey pants, he could never hide the fact that he was an outsider among the golden sons and daughters of Southern California. Jimmy later relished his role as loner, but it was something else to be hopelessly impelled toward it. He was the first teenager, the man who started it all, founder of the brotherhood of teen, dweller in the never-never-land of mope and glory – a moody bastard.

TONY PARSONS

He hated authority, and dared it to intrude on his undisciplined lifestyle. He fought a lone battle with the film studios, but from a position of strength, knowing that he was young and in demand. It was this same stubborn streak of individualism that drove him to test the limits of his physical capabilities, to find excitement in danger, and ultimately to lose his life. However, by dying young Dean transcended stardom and became a mythical figure to those of the age group he never got beyond, and to successive generations entering that age group.

TERENCE PETTIGREW

The whole time I worked with the man I never got a civil word out of him. He always seemed resentful about something.

ROCK HUDSON

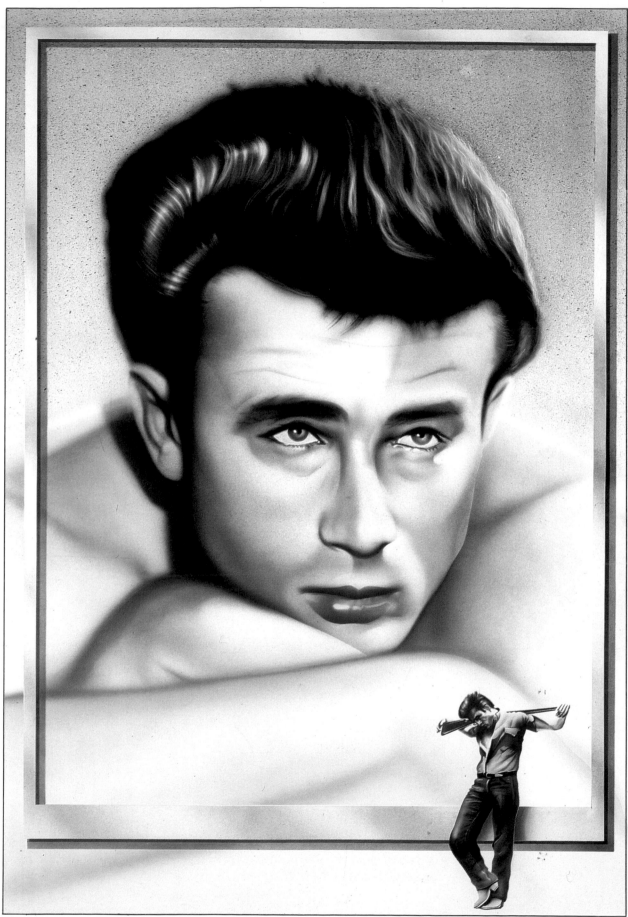

𝒥immy and I found we were a bit neurotic and had to justify our neurosis by creating, getting the pain out and sharing it.

DENNIS HOPPER

𝒮ulkily beautiful, he slunk around in jeans which were too tight, sneering and pouting and refusing to look adults in the eye, unloving and unlovable to them, because they either ignored him or substituted material goods for the understanding and loving acceptance he craved. His potency, though, was less in his youth than in the sadness and world-weariness he brought to his roles.

JULIE WELCH

*James Dean is indeed a perfect star; god, hero,
model. But this perfection, if it has only been able to
fulfil itself by means of the star system, derives from the
life and death of the real James Dean and from the
exigence which is his own as well as that of a generation
which sees itself in him, reflected and transfigured in
twin mirrors: screen and death.*

EDGAR MORIN

*Jimmy Dean started the entire youth movement. And
a lot of young people today, in looking back, realize –
even though they weren't even born when he died – that
he was the first rebel: he was the first guy to ask all the
questions: 'Why? Why?' He was the first one to give
teenagers an identification of any kind. Before Jimmy
Dean you were either a baby or you were a man. In
between was just one of those terrible stages that you
had to get out of rather quickly. And he didn't. He gave
the teenagers a status.*

SAL MINEO

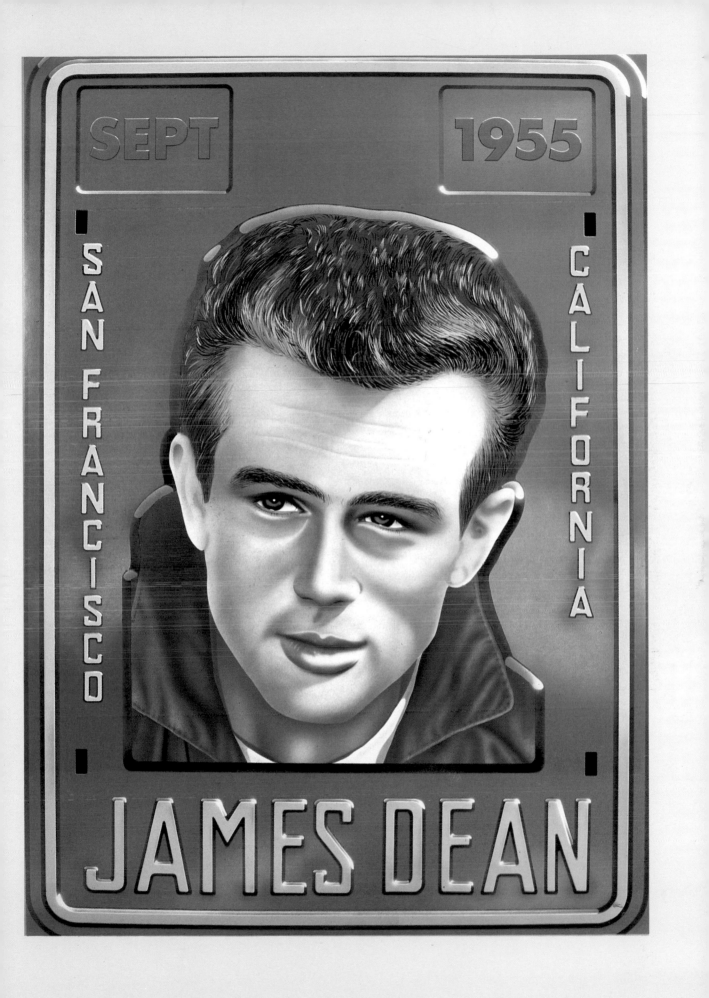

He carried preparation very, very far. I think he had a kind of pathological desire for tension.

LEONARD ROSENMAN

*H*e was like, say, an electric mixer — until it's plugged in it isn't functioning. Like a spiritual marriage with someone, it didn't matter who, male, female, young or old, or it may even be an animal, I don't know. But unless he felt really close — married to someone — he didn't function. He was just frantic until he found this feeling of togetherness with someone he loved and trusted.

MAILA 'VAMPIRA' NURMI

A beautiful face – desolate and strange and lonely, sensitive yet knowing, capable of unexpected sweetness and sudden violence. See the boy in East of Eden, *secretly spying on the innocent rompings of his nice brother and his equally nice girlfriend, Dean's face a combination of horror and longing. Watch him in* Rebel Without a Cause *cooling his face with a milk bottle straight from the icebox – he makes the pint of milk come alive; he uses it like a sex aid.*

TONY PARSONS

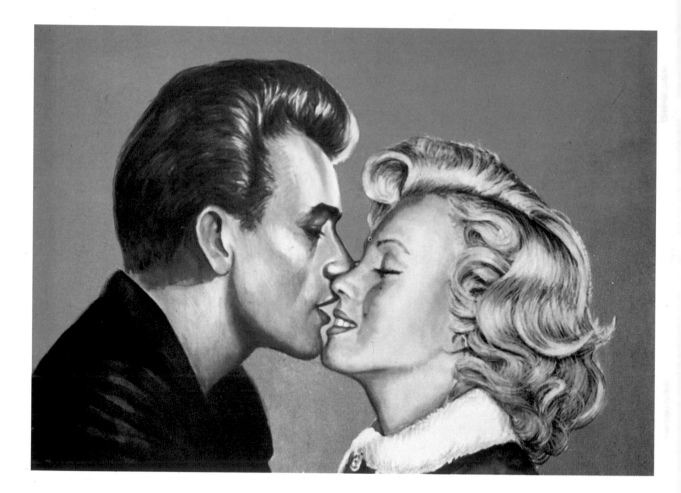

There's a lot of jealousy about Jimmy in terms of 'Why should he have all this adoration? Why should people still have a kind of thing about him?' Well, there are only two people in the world that I can remember, within my lifetime, that created that. One was Marilyn Monroe, and the other was James Dean. It's very funny – if you get four or five people around who knew Jim, everyone has a story to tell that they remember. Everyone has something to say about it. But if you put 'em all together, it almost sounds as if you're talking about four or five different people.

SAMMY DAVIS JR.

Where have all
the good Times gone?

When I was not on camera, I would watch George watching Jimmy. George would smile, but he didn't ever let Jimmy know he was fond of him.

ELIZABETH TAYLOR

I can see him now blinking behind his glasses after having been guilty of some preposterous bit of behaviour, and revealing by his very cast of defiance that he felt some sense of unworthiness.

GEORGE STEVENS

We were all trying to be individualists in such a devoted way. But I think that Jimmy didn't have to work at it. I think that he was actually an individualist among a group of individualists. He used to be at parties where the other actors where. Never say a word to anyone. If we were listening to music, he would sit in the corner and play his bongo drums: I don't think I ever remember him holding a conversation with anyone. Maybe a few words here and there.

CARROLL BAKER

*D*ean's personae are volatile amalgams of
rage and compassion alternating within the
barest fraction of a beat.

EDWARD S. SMALL

*E*ven if people didn't know who he was
they'd turn and look at him walking down
the street. I mean, no one walked like that in
those days.

JOE MASSOT

*J*immy had, in my estimation, a severe identity problem – he
really didn't know who he was. He certainly identified with the
roles that were given him, and I think that roles – these roles of
Cal and the rebellious boy in Rebel Without a Cause and the
rebellious ranch-hand in Giant – were given to him because he
was that to a degree. Except, there was a kind of an unfortunate
revolution in the closet, because he had no real identity himself.

LEONARD ROSENMAN

Moody young American actor who, after a brief build-up in small roles, was acclaimed as the image of the mid-'fifties; his tragic death in a car crash caused an astonishing worldwide outburst of emotional necrophilia. A phenomenon of the 'fifties, more popular dead than alive.

LESLIE HALLIWELL

I sometimes underestimated him and sometimes he overestimated the effects he thought he was getting. 'It's tough on you,' he'd seem to imply, 'but I've just got to do it this way.' From the director's angle, this isn't the most delightful sort of fellow to work with.

GEORGE STEVENS

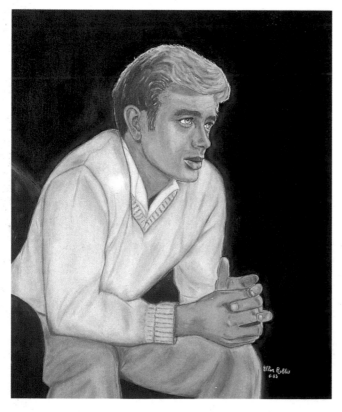

I think Dean died at the right time. Had he lived he would never have been able to keep up with all that publicity.

HUMPHREY BOGART

Jett was hardly a sympathetic guy, but he was the most real and perhaps the most understandable of Dean's three magnificent portraits.

GORDON GOW

The guy was guided by some inner light of his own. Maybe even he did not know what it was. I knew he had been motherless since early childhood and he missed a lot of love – I think he was still waiting for some lost tenderness.

GEORGE STEVENS

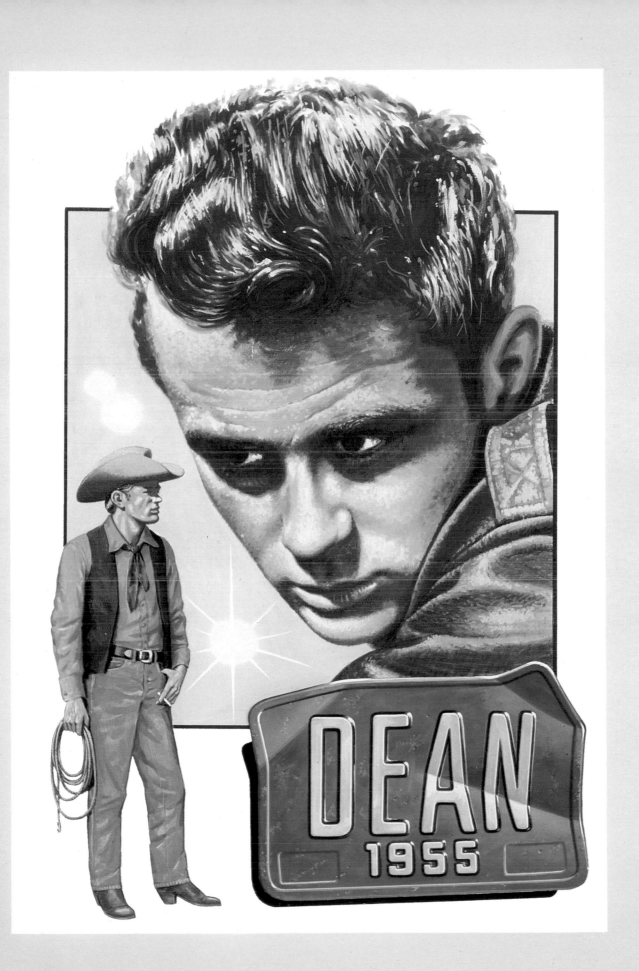

DEAN
1955

ean was never a friend of mine, but he had an idée fixe about me. Whatever I did, he did. He was always trying to get close to me. He used to call up. I'd listen to him talking to the answering service asking for me, leaving messages. But I never spoke up. I never called him back.

MARLON BRANDO

NORMAN PATTERSON '58

102

Jimmy used to call Montgomery Clift and say, 'I'm a great actor and you're my idol and I need to see you because I need to talk to you and I need to communicate', and Clift would change his phone number. Then, after Jimmy was dead, Clift saw all three of his films — and every time, he'd get drunk and cry about the fact that he'd denied this young man the opportunity of seeing and talking to him.

JULIE HARRIS

Jimmy was the most inventive actor that I've ever met. He was always thinking up marvellous movements and pieces of business, but they always fit in with the scene and the character.

CARROLL BAKER

I didn't like Dean particularly. He was hard to be around. He hated George Stevens, didn't think he was a good director, and he was always angry and full of contempt. He never smiled. He was sulky and had no manners.

ROCK HUDSON

Stevens and Dean feuded throughout the production, with Stevens complaining, 'Dean was not my choice for the role. He had the ability to take a scene and break it down . . . into so many bits and pieces that I couldn't see the scenes from the trees, so to speak. From a director's point of view that isn't the most delightful sort of fellow. All in all, it was a hell of a headache working with him.' By the time the picture was completed, the hostility between the two was so intense that Stevens publicly stated that 'Dean will never appear in another film I do.'

ALAN LADD

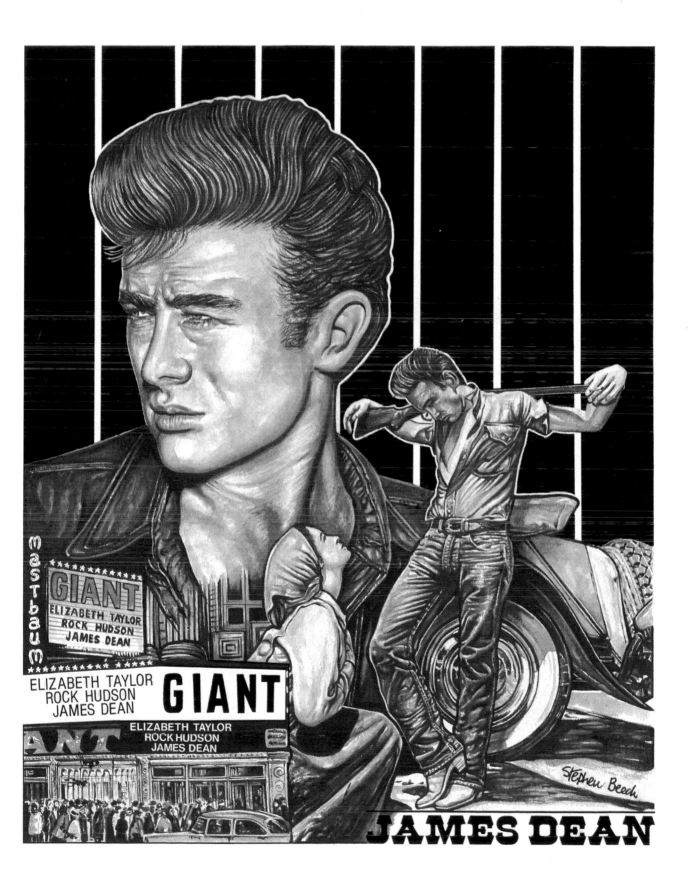

GIANT
ELIZABETH TAYLOR
ROCK HUDSON
JAMES DEAN

ELIZABETH TAYLOR
ROCK HUDSON
JAMES DEAN
GIANT

ELIZABETH TAYLOR
ROCK HUDSON
JAMES DEAN

Stephen Beech

JAMES DEAN

In James Dean youth found a heroic celebration of the anarchy and the ecstasy of being young. His death was the perfect punchline to his life and work. James Dean is living and dying proof that there is an alternative to growing up and old and getting tame and embarrassing. You get out – and you get buried – when you are right on top. His moves are aped in the street by kids who weren't born when his corpse was already ten years old.

TONY PARSONS

I think he loved life. I think he may have grabbed too strongly at life, but I don't think he had a death wish.

NATALIE WOOD

James Dean! James Dean!
I know just what you mean.
James Dean, you said it all so clean!
And I know my life would look all right
if I could see it on the silver screen.
You were a low-down rebel if there ever was
even if you had no cause!
You may talk about a lowdown maverick
'frigerator, you were just too cool for school,
Sock hops, soda pop, basketball and all those
shots.
The only thing that got you off was
breaking all the rules!
James Dean! James Dean!
So hungry and so mean!
Little James Dean, up on the screen.
Wondering who he might be.
Along came a spider and tripped up a rider,
and took him down the road to eternity.
James Dean! James Dean!
We bought it sight unseen!
You were too fast to live
and too young to die, bye, bye!

THE EAGLES

In the autumn of 1955 I went to Los Angeles to make my first Hollywood film . . . Thelma Moss . . . had said she wished to take me out to dinner my first night in town. We arrived at three restaurants of repute . . . and finally settled for a delightful little Italian bistro. When we got there . . . there was no table available. As we walked disconsolately away I said, 'I don't care where we eat or what. Just something, somewhere.' I became aware of running, sneakered feet behind us and turned to face a fair young man in sweat-shirt and blue jeans.

'You want a table?' he asked. 'Join me. My name is James Dean.' We followed him gratefully, but on the way back to the restaurant he turned into a car-park saying, 'I'd like to show you something.' Among the other cars there was what looked like a large shiny, silver parcel wrapped in cellophane and tied with ribbon. 'It's just been delivered,' he said, with bursting pride. 'I haven't even driven it yet.' The sportscar looked sinister to me, although it had a large bunch of red carnations resting on the bonnet.

'How fast is it?' I asked.

'She'll do a hundred and fifty,' he replied.

Exhausted, hungry, feeling a little ill-tempered in spite of Dean's kindness, I heard myself saying in a voice I could hardly recognize as my own, 'Please never get in it.' I looked at my watch. 'It is now ten o'clock, Friday the 23rd of September, 1955. If you get in that car you will be found dead in it by this time next week.'

He laughed. 'Oh, shucks! Don't be so mean!' . . .

We parted an hour later, full of smiles. No further reference was made to the wrapped-up car . . . In my heart I was uneasy with myself. At four o'clock in the afternoon of the following Friday James Dean was dead, killed while driving the car.

ALEC GUINNESS

DEAN · THE·LAST·JOURNEY

He had it coming to him. The way he drove he had it coming to him.

GEORGE STEVENS

Jimmy was absolutely suicidal with a car. People just stayed away because they didn't want to get killed. I'm not saying that he wasn't gifted as a race-car driver, but that extra irresponsible attitude towards his own life, I think, influenced his winning very often.

LEONARD ROSENMAN

He was only 24, but what he achieved, and what he left behind him, will never be repeated. James Dean is a legend, remembered for simply playing himself. His passion for fast cars and bikes was not, as some may think, a passing whim. He had a burning desire to drive fast; he had owned other cars, and driven them the same way. He was young, he was successful, and he was good-looking; but he lived life differently to other people, he cut it fine.

BEKI ADAM

The night he was killed I was having dinner with a lot of his friends – Sal Mineo, Dick Davalos, Nick Adams. We were talking about Jimmy's lifestyle and Nick ventured the opinion that Jimmy wouldn't live till thirty. We pooh-poohed the idea. Later, when we finished eating, Nick and Sal walked me to my hotel. I was still under age then with a studio chaperone, and it was she who heard the news. She told Nick and Sal and asked them not to say anything to me because I had an early call the next day and she wanted me to sleep. So they left rather abruptly. Next morning the chaperone had to tell me because down in the lobby the newspapers had it on all the headlines. I didn't believe it. I think I stood at the window staring out for a long time. I went to work in a state of shock.

NATALIE WOOD

*A*merica has known many rebellions — but never one like this: millions of teenage rebels heading for nowhere, some in 'hot rod' cars, others on the blare of rock 'n' roll music, some with guns in their hands. At their head — a dead Leader.

PICTURE POST

GOODTIMES ENTERPRISES PRODUCTION

JAMES DEAN

THE FIRST AMERICAN TEENAGER

A FILM BY RAY CONNOLLY
PRODUCED BY
DAVID PUTTNAM AND SANDY LIEBERSON
NARRATED BY STACY KEACH

*I*t wasn't until 1955 that Hollywood was able to gratify a huge youth fantasy and come up with an all-purpose compendium of bad teen. James Dean was, of course, the embodiment of the whole deal. Montgomery Clift's vulnerability on one side and Brando's narrow-eyed tough on the other acted like twin John the Baptists to Dean's confused 'fifties Cool Jesus. Without a doubt, his best long-term career move was to die young and unsullied.

MICK FARREN

MAXELL. THE TAPE THAT LASTS AS LONG AS THE LEGEND.

He was inarticulate and eloquent. A generation of adolescent rebellion expressed in surly manners and sensitive speech. He left behind a small but remarkable legacy of work. At Maxell, we help you preserve his films, with tapes that are manufactured up to 60% above industry standards. Tapes that will deliver the same great quality and clarity after 500 plays. So as long as there are rebels without causes there will be the movies of James Dean to reflect their struggles and light their ways.

I think had he lived he would probably have surpassed anybody that we have in the motion picture industry today.

PAUL NEWMAN

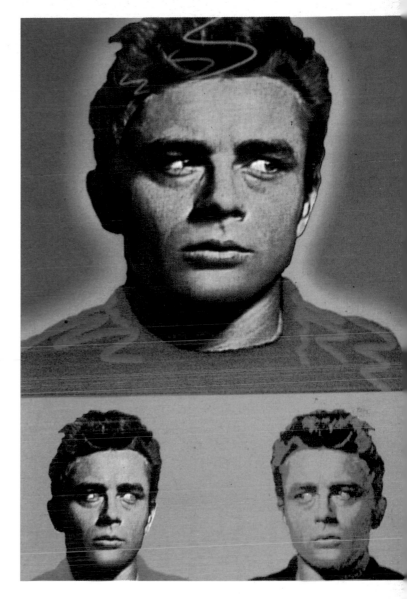

*H*is death caused a loss in the movie world that our industry could ill afford. Had he lived long enough I feel he would have made some incredible films; he had a sensitivity and a capacity to express emotion.

GARY COOPER

*W*hen I worked with him on TV I found him to be an intelligent young actor who seemed to live only for his work. He was completely dedicated and although a shy person he could hold a good conversation on many wide-ranging subjects.

RONALD REAGAN

He was fun to hang around with, but he was always making romance with his own activities. He made romance out of the fact that he didn't eat or dress like other people. Sometimes I felt that he was writing a biography about himself, you know, and that moment was entitled, 'This is the way Jimmy prepared for his role in . . . .

ROY SCHATT

We cannot speak of cinema without mentioning the name of James Dean, the freshly plucked 'fleur du mal'; James Dean, who is the cinema in the same sense as Lillian Gish, Chaplin, Ingrid Bergman, etc. He was the child who goes to a secret corner and refuses to speak. The rejection of a generation of Americans in the eyes of one youth.

MARCEAU DEVILLERS

I've always been a cinematic archaeologist and I didn't take the notice I should have done of James Dean.

KEVIN BROWNLOW

Jimmy had the temperament of a really versatile actor. I think, if he'd lived, he'd have been one of the finest.

JULIE HARRIS

JAMES DEAN, BOBBY SOX IDOL, KILLED IN $7000 CAR CRASH

the ANGELS ·Took Him ·For A FRIEND

LIVE FAST DIE YOUNG
HAVE A BEAUTIFUL CORPSE

*There is nothing much deader
than a dead motion picture actor, and yet,
even after James Dean had been some years dead,
    when they filed out of the close darkness
and the breathedout air of the second and third
and fourth run motion picture theatres
where they'd been seeing James Dean's old films,
they still lined up:
    the boys in the jackboots and the leather jackets,
the boys in the skintight jeans, the boys in broad
motorbike belts, before the mirrors in the restroom
to look at themselves and see James Dean;
    the resentful hair, the deep eyes
floating in lonesomeness, the bitter beat look,
the scorn on the lip . . .
    The girls flocked out dizzy with wanting
to run their fingers through his hair,
to feel that thwarted maleness; girl-boy almost,
but he needs a shave . . .
'Just him and me in the back seat of a car.'
    Their fathers snort, but sometimes they remember:
    'Nobody understood me either. I might have amounted
to something if the folks had understood.'
The older women struggle from their seats weteyed.*

JOHN DOS PASSOS

124

Acknowledgements

Illustrations

Dean by Steve Gulbis/Meiklejohn Graphics Limited: front cover, 109

Spirit of Dean by Mike Shaw: 95

The Rebel Without a Cause by Stephen Beech/The Beech Collection: 6

Internal Infant by Mike Shaw: 8

Gaintspawn by Mike Shaw: 5

Unbroken Umbilical by Mike Shaw: 13

Well Then: There Now by Mike Shaw: 26

Different Drum by Mike Shaw: 29

Ivan Van Der Walt/Universal Art: 30

The Torn Poster by Kenneth Kendall/collection of the artist: 35

James Dean, Nostalgie by Michelangeli/Naifs et Primitifs: 33

Ellen Robles: 36, 77, 98

September Sundown by Mike Shaw: 37

James Dean/Arti Grafiche Ricordi, S.p.A.: 38

James Dean, Poursuite by Michel Fauré/Naifs et Primitifs: 39

Leslie Dutton/collection of the artist: 40, 74, 80

Feline Fenêtre by Mike Shaw: 41

See the Jaguar by Kenneth Kendall/collection of the artist: 42

James Dean by Geoff Kelly/Wizard & Genius – Idealdecor: 43

James Dean by Scott Wilson/Michael Woodward Licensing: 44

James Dean, Hero by Michel Fauré/Naifs et Primitifs: 45

James Dean Evasion by Michel Fauré/Naifs et Primitifs: 46

Welcome to the Club!/Panache Studio – Hallmark Cards Limited: 47

Irene Inman/collection of the artist: 48, 56, 69

James by F. Dupuich/Editions François Nugeron: 49

September 30, 1955 by Jan Hunt/Verkerke GmbH: 50–1

Salinas Shalom by Mike Shaw: 52

Lance Collins/Star Portraits: 53, 60

James Dean by Kenneth Kendall/collection of the artist: 55

Centre Frame by Mike Shaw: 57

Norman Patterson/Universal Art: 58, 102, 128

Dean by Rob Fleming/Talep Associates: 61

Androgynous Americana by Mike Shaw: 62

East of Eden by Kenneth Kendall/collection of the artist: 63

James Dean by Saeko Tsuemura/Wizard & Genius – Idealdecor: 64

James Dean, Incompris by Michel Fauré/Naifs et Primitifs: 65

R. W. Richards/collection of David Loehr: 66

James Dean, Seul dans la Ville by Michel Fauré/ Naifs et Primitifs: 67

Quotations

The Little Prince Antoine de Saint-Exupéry, pub. William Heinemann Limited and Editions Gallimard, Paris: 7, 9

East of Eden © Warner Bros.: 17

Rebel Without a Cause © Warner Bros.: 20

Giant © Warner Bros.: 23

Films & Filming, pub. Plusloop Limited: (October 1965) 33 (top), 50 (bottom), 121 (top); (October 1975) 34 (bottom); (August 1977) 45 (centre); (September 1985) 59 (top); (October 1985) 88 (top)

Cahiers du Cinema, British Film Institute Publishing: 31

Biographic Dictionary of the Cinema, David Thomson, pub. Martin Secker & Warburg Limited: 34 (top)

James Dean: the First American Teenager, Goodtimes Enterprises – David Puttnam and Sandy Lieberson: 37 (bottom), 62 (top), 65 (top), 70 (bottom), 81 (top), 88 (bottom), 90–1, 92 (bottom), 94 (bottom), 97 (bottom), 103 (centre), 106 (bottom), 113

Revolt in Style, George Melly, by permission of A.M. Heath & Co. Limited: 39 (top)

The Way It Was, Terry Cunningham, pub. Stagedoor: 39 (bottom), 41 (centre), 50 (top), 56, 74 (centre), 77 (bottom), 78 (centre), 85 (bottom), 98 (bottom), 100 (bottom), 121 (centre, bottom)

The Warner Brothers Story, Clive Hirschhorn, pub. Octopus Books Limited: 41 (top)

The Rebel Hero in Films, Joe Morella, pub. Citadel Press, Inc.: 41 (bottom), 78 (top)

Marlon Brando, the Only Contender, Gary Carey, pub. Robson Books Limited: 42 (top), 58

James Dean Is Not Dead, Steven Morrissey, pub. Babylon Books; distributed by International Music Publications: 42 (centre, bottom), 45 (bottom), 65 (bottom), 69, 78 (bottom), 87 (top), 94 (top, centre), 97 (centre), 98 (centre), 102, 103 (top, bottom), 112, 116, 122 (top)

James Dean on Location, Marceau Devillers, pub. Sidgwick & Jackson Limited: 45 (top), 122 (above centre)

The Black Leather Jacket, Mick Farren, pub. Plexus Publishing Limited: 46, 118 (bottom)

James Dean: a Poster Book, Philip Harvey, pub. Atlanta Press Limited: 52, 59 (bottom), 74 (bottom)

The Hit, Tony Parsons, pub. Holborn Publishing Group: 60, 81 (bottom), 92 (top), 106 (top)

James Dean, Roger St Pierre, pub. Anabas Books: 62 (top), 77 (top) 118 (top)

Hollywood in the 'Fifties, Gordon Gow, pub. Tantivy Press Limited: distributed by Zwemmer: 62 (bottom), 100 (top), 122 (bottom)

A Hundred Different Lives, Raymond Massey, pub. Robson Books Limited: 67

The Radio Times, Terence Pettigrew, pub. BBC Enterprises Limited: 70 (top), 85 (top)

Superstars, Alexander Walker, pub. Phaidon Limited: 72

The Cornerhouse, Adam Faith, pub. Cornerhouse Limited: 74 (top)

Leading Men, Julie Welch, pub. Conran Octopus Limited: 87 (bottom)

Films and Filmmakers: Vol. 3 (Actors and Actresses), ed. James Vinson, pub. St James Press: 97 (top)

The Filmgoer's Companion, Leslie Halliwell, pub. Grafton Books: 98 (top)

Ladd, Beverley Linet, pub. Robson Books Limited: 104

'James Dean', words and music J. Browne, G. Frey, J.D. Souter, Don Henley, © Benchmark Music/Warner Bros. Music Limited: 109

Blessings in Disguise, Alec Guinness, pub. Hamish Hamilton Limited: 110

Star Cars, Beki Adam, pub. Osprey Publishing Limited: 115